# ACTING

## THE FIRST SIX LESSONS

BY

RICHARD BOLESLAVSKY

Martino Publishing
Mansfield Centre, CT
2013

*Martino Publishing*
*P.O. Box 373,*
*Mansfield Centre, CT 06250 USA*


ISBN  978-1-61427-433-9


© *2013  Martino Publishing*

Cover design by T. Matarazzo

*Printed in the United States of America On 100% Acid-Free Paper*

# ACTING

## THE FIRST SIX LESSONS

BY

RICHARD BOLESLAVSKY

FOR

NATIONAL THEATRE CONFERENCE

THEATRE ARTS INC.

NEW YORK

PRINTED IN THE UNITED STATES OF AMERICA
BY J. J. LITTLE AND IVES COMPANY, NEW YORK

*Introduction*

THE *Way of the Lancer* brought immediate literary acclaim to Richard Boleslavski, spelled with an "i" after the manner of his Polish ancestors. The book was variously called a work of genius, the best human document of the events preceding the Russian Revolution, a masterly narrative biography, a new writing of history. But no matter what else critics said of it, they almost invariably added that it was intensely dramatic, obviously the work of a mind trained in the theatre. As rightly they might say, for the uniform of an officer of the Polish Lancers and the change from "y" to "i" was no disguise for Richard Boleslavsky, an actor of the Moscow Art Theatre, Director of the Moscow Art Theatre Studio and, in America, Director of the Laboratory Theatre, of many successful plays on Broadway, of films at Hollywood.

What many of the critics seemed to miss, however, in this splendid book and its sequel, *Lances Down*, was the fact that Boleslavsky's style and point of view, dramatic as it undoubtedly was, had little to do with the art of the writer of plays. *Way of the Lancer* was not the product of a dramatist's mind, turned narrator, but of an actor's mind. One is almost the converse of the other. The actor is usually word-shy and inarticulate. Often he does not know what it is he does or how he does it, that makes him an actor. Even when he knows, it is difficult for him to say it or write it. He can only express it in action. His language is a language of movement, of gesture, of voice, of the creation and projection of character by things done or left undone. The dramatist, on the other hand, works easily with words, writes fluently, interprets character, situation, and events, manner and method in his own terms. So far as the art and the craft of acting have been written of at all, it is usually the dramatist or the critic who has written of them. That is why there is so little in print really to explain the actor to himself and to his fellows.

Talma, Fanny Kemble, Coquelin and, among the moderns, Louis Calvert and Stanislavsky stand out as actors who have tried to interpret acting. But Stanislavsky's fine contribution is welded into the text of his autobiography, *My Life in Art*, and all the rest are, generally speaking, an effort to create a philosophy of acting rather than to analyze the elements of the art of acting or to establish a technique for the player. Must an actor have experienced an emotion

6

to portray it; will he portray it better if he actually renews the feeling every time he assumes it; shall acting be far removed from life, or as close to it as possible? Such are the problems these actor-philosophers set themselves to solve. And with the illustrations drawn from high experience, their writings have greatly illumined the field. They have clarified the fundamental laws of the art for many artists. But they do not help an actor to learn the elements of his craft.

So that, in a way, these essays of Boleslavsky's, these *First Lessons in Acting*, in dialogue form, stand alone in their field. Gayly as they are told, there is not a word in any of them that is not seriously to the point, that is not calculated, out of long years of work and study as an actor and as a director in the professional and in the art theatre, to help a young actor on his way. They actually select his tools for him and show him how to use them. And that is a grateful task. For while an actor's tools are all within his own body and mind and spirit, they are by their very nearness harder to isolate and put to special use than tools of wood and iron. Concentration and observation, experience and memory, movement and poise, creation and projection—an actor must make them all the servants of his talent.

In an article he wrote some years ago on the *Fundamentals of Acting*, Boleslavsky himself defined the field he covers here. "The actor's art," he said, "cannot be taught. He must be born with ability; but the technique, through which his talent can find expression—that can and must be taught. An appreciation of this fact is of the utmost importance, not only to students of acting but to every actor who is interested in the perfection of his art. For, after all, technique is something which is perfectly realistic and quite possible to make one's own."

The basis of this technique, the mere development of the actor's physical resources, although he recognizes and stresses its importance, is not what Boleslavsky calls "technique". The training of the body he likens rather to the tuning up of an instrument. "Even the most perfectly tuned violin," he goes on to say, "will not play by itself, without the musician to make it sing. The equipment of the ideal actor . . . is not complete unless he has . . . the technique of an 'emotion maker' or creator; unless he can follow the advice of Joseph Jefferson to 'Keep your heart warm and your head cool'. Can it be done? Most certainly! It is merely necessary to think of life as an unbroken sequence of two different kinds of steps. . . . Problem steps and Action steps. . . . The first step is for the actor to understand what the problem is that confronts him. Then the spark of the will pushes him toward dynamic action. . . . When an actor realizes that the solution of a certain part may consist merely in being able first, to stand on the stage for perhaps no more than one-five-hundredth of a second, cool-headed and firm of purpose, aware of the problem before him; and then in the next one-five-hundredth of a second or, it may be, five or ten seconds, to precipitate himself intensely into the action which the situation requires, he will have achieved the perfect technique of acting."

First to know rightly what to do, and then to do it rightly. That is all. It seems little enough. But it is not by chance that Boleslavsky puts the visits of *The Creature*, who is the subject of these lessons, months, sometimes years, apart. He is thinking practically, not wishfully. He knows the length of the road she will need to travel between lessons. He knows that in acting more than in any other art a little less than good is worlds away from good. An actor cannot be made between luncheon and dinner. He accepts the fact that the profession may take a lifetime of work and that it is a profession well worth the work of a lifetime.

EDITH J. R. ISAACS

*New York,*
*February, 1933.*

# ACTING

## THE FIRST SIX LESSONS

# CONTENTS

*Introduction*                                          5

*The First Lesson:* CONCENTRATION                       15

*The Second Lesson:* MEMORY OF EMOTION                  29

*The Third Lesson:* DRAMATIC ACTION                     49

*The Fourth Lesson:* CHARACTERIZATION                   65

*The Fifth Lesson:* OBSERVATION                         89

*The Sixth Lesson:* RHYTHM                             103

# THE FIRST LESSON

## Concentration

*orning. My room. A knock at the door.*

M I: Come in. *(The door opens, slowly and timidly. Enter a Pretty Creature of eighteen. She looks at me with wide-open, frightened eyes and crushes her handbag violently.)*

THE CREATURE: I . . . I . . . I hear that you teach dramatic art.

I: No! I am sorry. Art cannot be taught. To possess an art means to possess talent. That is something one has or has not. You can develop it by hard work, but to create a talent is impossible. What I do is to help those who have decided to work on the stage, to develop and to educate themselves for honest and conscientious work in the theatre.

THE CREATURE: Yes, of course. Please help me. I simply love the theatre.

I: Loving the theatre is not enough. Who does not love it? To consecrate oneself to the theatre, to devote one's entire life to it, give it all one's thought, all one's emotions! For the sake of the theatre to give up everything, to suffer everything! And more important than all, to be ready to give the theatre everything—your entire being—expecting the theatre to give you nothing in return, not the least grain of what seemed to you so beautiful in it and so alluring.

THE CREATURE: I know. I played a great deal at school. I understand that the theatre brings suffering. I am not afraid of it. I am ready for anything if I can only play, play, play.

I: And suppose the theatre does not want you to play and play and play?

THE CREATURE: Why shouldn't it?

I: Because it might not find you talented.

THE CREATURE: But when I played at school. . . .

I: What did you play?

THE CREATURE: *King Lear.*

I: What part did you play in this trifle?

THE CREATURE: King Lear himself. And all my friends and our professor of literature and even Aunt Mary told me I played wonderfully and that I certainly had talent.

I: Pardon me, I don't mean to criticize the nice people whom you name, but are you sure that they are connoisseurs of talent?

THE CREATURE: Our professor is very strict. He himself worked with me on King Lear. He is a great authority.

I: I see, I see. And Aunt Mary?

THE CREATURE: She met Mr. Belasco personally.

I: So far, so good. But can you tell me how your professor, when working on King Lear, wanted you to play these lines, for instance: "Blow winds, and crack your cheeks! Rage! Blow!"

THE CREATURE: Do you want me to play it for you?

I: No. Just tell me how you learned to read those lines. What were you trying to attain?

THE CREATURE: I had to stand this way, my feet well together, incline my body forward a little, lift my head like this, stretch out my arms to heaven and shake my fists. Then I had to take a deep breath and burst into sarcastic laughter—ha! ha! ha! *(She laughs, a charming, childish laugh. Only at happy eighteen can one laugh that way.)* Then, as though cursing heaven, as loud as possible pronounce the words: "Blow winds and crack your cheeks! Rage! Blow!"

I: Thank you, that is quite enough for a clear understanding of the part of King Lear, as well as for a definition of your talent. May I ask you one more thing? Will you, if you please, say this sentence, first cursing the heavens and then without cursing them. Just keep the sense of the phrase—only its thought. *(She doesn't think long, she is accustomed to curse heaven.)*

THE CREATURE: When you curse the heavens, you say it this way: "Blooooow wiiiiinds, and Craaaaack your cheeks, Raaaaage Blooooow." *(The Creature tries very hard to curse the heavens but through the window I see the azure heavens laughing at the curse. I do the same.)* And without cursing them, I must do it some other way. Well . . . I don't know how . . . Isn't it funny? Well, this way: *(The Creature becomes confused and, with a charming smile, swallowing the words, hurriedly pronounces them all on one note.)* "Blowwindsandcrackyourcheeksrageblow." *(She becomes completely confused and tries to destroy her handbag. A pause.)*

I: How strange! You are so young; you do not hesitate a second before cursing heaven. Yet you are unable to speak these words simply and plainly, to show their inner meaning. You want to play a Chopin Nocturne without knowing where the notes are. You grimace, you mutilate the words of the poet and eternal emotion, and at the same time you do not possess the most elemental quality of a literate man— an ability to transmit the thoughts, feelings, and words of another logically. What right have you to say that you have worked in the theatre? You have destroyed the very conception of the word Theatre. *(A pause; the Creature looks at me with the eyes of one innocently condemned to death. The little handbag lies on the floor.)*

THE CREATURE: So I must never play?

I: And if I say *Never?* *(Pause. The eyes of the Creature change their expression, she looks straight into my soul with a sharp scrutinizing look, and seeing that I am not joking, clenches her teeth, and tries in vain to hide what is happening in her soul. But it is no use. One enormous real tear rolls out of her eye, and the Creature at that moment becomes dear to me. It spoils my intentions completely. She controls herself, clenches her teeth, and says in a low voice—)*

THE CREATURE: But I am going to play. I have nothing else in my life. *(At eighteen they always talk that way. But just the same I am deeply touched.)*

I: All right then. I must tell you that this very moment you did more for the theatre, or rather for yourself in the theatre, than you did in playing all your parts. You suffered just now; you felt deeply. Those are two things without which you cannot do in any art and especially in the art of the theatre. Only by paying this price can you attain the happiness of creation, the happiness of the birth of a new artistic value. To prove that, let us work together right now. Let us try to create a small, but real, artistic value according to your strength. It will be the first step in

19

your development as an actress. *(The enormous, beautiful tear is forgotten. It disappeared somewhere into space. A charming, happy smile appears instead. I never thought my creaking voice could produce such a change.)*

Listen and answer sincerely. Have you ever seen a man, a specialist, busy on some creative problem in the course of his work? A pilot on an ocean liner, for instance, responsible for thousands of lives, or a biologist working at his microscope, or an architect working out the plan of a complicated bridge, or a great actor seen from the wings during his interpretation of a fine part?

THE CREATURE: I saw John Barrymore from the wings when he was playing *Hamlet*.

I: What impressed you chiefly as you watched him?

THE CREATURE: He was *marvelous!!!*

I: I know that, but what else?

THE CREATURE: He paid no attention to me.

I: That is more important; not only not to you but to nothing around him. He was acting in his work as the pilot would, the scientist, or the architect—he was concentrating. Remember this word *Concentrate*. It is important in every art and especially in the art of the theatre. Concentration is the quality which permits us to direct all our spiritual and intellectual forces towards one definite object and to continue as long as it pleases us to do so—sometimes for a time much

20

longer than our physical strength can endure. I knew a fisherman once who, during a storm, did not leave his rudder for forty-eight hours, concentrating to the last minute on his work of steering his schooner. Only when he had brought the schooner back safely into the harbor did he allow his body to faint. This strength, this certainty of power over yourself, is the fundamental quality of every creative artist. You must find it within yourself, and develop it to the last degree.

THE CREATURE: But how?

I: I will tell you. Don't hurry. The most important thing is that in the art of the theatre a special kind of concentration is needed. The pilot has a compass, the scientist has his microscope, the architect his drawings —all external, visible objects of concentration and creation. They have, so to speak, a *material* aim, to which all their force is directed. So has a sculptor, a painter, a musician, an author. But it is quite different with the actor. Tell me, what do you think is the object of his concentration?

THE CREATURE: His part.

I: Yes, until he learns it. But it is only after studying and rehearsing that the actor *starts* to create. Or rather let us say that at first he creates "searchingly" and on the opening night he begins to create "constructively" in his acting. And what is acting?

THE CREATURE: Acting? Acting is when he . . . acts, acts . . . I don't know.

I: You want to consecrate all your life to a task without knowing what it is? Acting is *the life of the human soul receiving its birth through art*. In a creative theatre the object for an actor's concentration is the *human soul*. In the first period of his work—the searching—the object for concentration is his own soul and those of the men and women who surround him. In the second period—the constructive one—only his own soul. Which means that, to act, you must know how to concentrate on something materially imperceptible,—on something which you can perceive only by penetrating deeply into your own entity, recognizing what would be evidenced in life only in a moment of the greatest emotion and most violent struggle. In other words, you need a spiritual concentration on emotions which do not exist, but are invented or imagined.

THE CREATURE: But how can one develop in oneself something which does not exist. How can one start?

I: From the very beginning. Not from a Chopin Nocturne but from the simplest scales. Such scales are your five senses: sight, hearing, smell, touch and taste. They will be the key of your creation like a scale for a Chopin Nocturne. Learn how to govern this scale, how with your entire being to concentrate on your senses, to make them work artificially, to give them different problems and create the solutions.

# CONCENTRATION

THE CREATURE: I hope you don't mean to say that I don't even know how to listen or how to feel.

I: In life you may know. Nature has taught you a little. *(She becomes very daring and speaks as though challenging the whole world.)*

THE CREATURE: No, on the stage, too.

I: Is that so? Let us see. Please, just as you are sitting now, listen to the scratching of an imaginary mouse in that corner.

THE CREATURE: Where is the audience?

I: That doesn't concern you in the least. Your audience is in no hurry as yet to buy tickets for your performance. Forget about it. Do the problem I give you. Listen to the scratching of a mouse in that corner.

THE CREATURE: All right. *(There follows a helpless gesture with the right and then the left ear which has nothing in common with listening to the delicate scratching of a mouse's paw in the silence.)*

I: All right. Now please listen to a symphony orchestra playing the march from *Aida*. You know the march?

THE CREATURE: Of course.

I: Please. *(The same business follows—nothing to do with listening to a triumphal march. I smile. The Creature begins to understand that something is wrong, and becomes confused. She awaits my verdict.)* I see you recognize how helpless you are, how little you see the difference between the lower *do* and the higher *do*.

THE CREATURE: You give me a very difficult problem.

I: Is it easier to curse the heavens in *King Lear?* No, my dear, I must tell you frankly: You do not know how to create the smallest, simplest bit of the life of the human soul. You do not know how to *concentrate spiritually*. Not only do you not know how to create complicated feelings and emotions but you do not even possess your own senses. All of that you must learn by hard daily exercises of which I can give you thousands. If you think, you will be able to invent another thousand.

THE CREATURE: All right. I will learn. I will do everything you tell me. Will I be an actress then?

I: I am glad you ask. Of course you will not be an actress, yet. To listen and to look and to feel truly is not all. You must do all that in a hundred ways. Suppose that you are playing. The curtain goes up and your first problem is to listen to the sound of a departing car. You must do it in such a way that the thousand people in the theatre who at that moment are each concentrating on some particular object—one on the stock exchange, one on home worries, one on politics, one on a dinner or the pretty girl in the next chair—in such a way that they know and feel immediately that their concentration is less important than yours, though you are concentrating only on the sound of a departing imaginary car. They must feel they have not the right to think of the stock exchange in the presence of your imaginary car! That you are more powerful than they, that, for the moment, you are the most important person in the world, and nobody dares disturb you. Nobody dares to disturb a painter at his work, and it is the actor's own fault if he allows the public to interfere with his creation. If all actors would possess the concentration and the knowledge of which I speak, this would never happen.

THE CREATURE: But what does he need for that?

I: Talent and technique. The education of an actor consists of three parts. The first is the education of his body, the whole physical apparatus, of every muscle and sinew. As a director I can manage very well with an actor with a completely developed body.

THE CREATURE: What time must a young actor spend on this?

I: An hour and a half daily on the following exercises: gymnastics, rhythmic gymnastics, classical and interpretive dancing, fencing, all kinds of breathing exercises, voice-placing exercises, diction, singing, pantomime, make-up. An hour and a half a day for two years with steady practice afterwards in what you have acquired will make an actor *pleasing to look at.*

The second part of the education is intellectual, cultural. One can discuss Shakespeare, Molière, Goethe, and Calderon only with a cultured actor who knows what these men stand for and what has been done in the theatres of the world to produce their plays. I need an actor who knows the world's literature and who can see the difference between German and French Romanticism. I need an actor who knows the history of painting, of sculpture and of music, who can always carry in his mind, at least approximately, the style of every period, and the individuality of every great painter. I need an actor who has a fairly clear idea of the psychology of motion, of psychoanalysis, of the expression of emotion, and the logic of feeling. I need an actor who knows something of the anatomy of the human body, as well as of the great works of sculpture. All this knowledge is necessary because the actor comes in contact with these things, and has to work with them on the stage. This intellectual training would make an actor who could play a great variety of parts.

The third kind of education, the beginning of which I showed you today, is the education and training of the soul—the most important factor of dramatic action. An actor cannot exist without a soul developed enough to be able to accomplish, at the first command of the will, every action and change stipulated. In other words, the actor must have a soul capable of living through any situation demanded by the author. There is no great actor without such a soul. Unfortunately it is acquired by long, hard work, at great expense of time and experience, and through a series of experimental parts. The work for this consists in the development of the following faculties: complete possession of all the five senses in various imaginable situations; development of a memory of feeling, memory of inspiration or penetration, memory of imagination, and, last, a visual memory.

THE CREATURE: But I have never heard of all those.

I: Yet they are almost as simple as "cursing the heavens". The development of faith in imagination; the development of the imagination itself; the development of naiveté; the development of observation; the development of will power; the development of the capacity to give variety in the expression of emotion; the development of the sense of humor and the tragic sense. Nor is this all.

THE CREATURE: Is it possible?

I: One thing alone remains which cannot be developed but must be present. It is *TALENT*. *(The Creature sighs and falls into deep meditation. I also sit in silence.)*

THE CREATURE: You make the theatre seem like something very big, very important, very . . . . .

I: Yes, for me the theatre is a great mystery, a mystery in which are wonderfully wedded the two eternal phenomena, the dream of *Perfection* and the dream of the *Eternal*. Only to such a theatre is it worth while to give one's life. *(I get up, the Creature looks at me with sorrowful eyes. I understand what these eyes express.)*

# THE SECOND LESSON

## *Memory of Emotion*

You remember the lovely creature who came to me a year ago, and "simply *loved* the theatre"? She came back this winter. She entered the room quietly and with grace, smiling, her face aglow.

THE CREATURE: Hello!

*(Her handclasp was firm and strong; her eyes looked straight into mine; her figure was well balanced and controlled; what a difference!)*

I: How do you do? I am certainly glad to see you. I have followed your work although you did not come back to me. I never thought that you would come back. I thought I had frightened you the last time.

THE CREATURE: Oh, no, you didn't! But you certainly gave me a lot to work on, an awful lot. What a horrible time I have had with that idea of concentration. Everybody laughed at me—Once I was nearly run down by a street car because I had tried too effectively to concentrate on "the happiness of my existence". You see, I give myself problems like that for exercise, exactly as you told me to do. In this particular case, I was fired from my job and I wanted to pretend to myself that it didn't concern me at all. And I succeeded. Oh, I was stronger than ever. I was on my way home and made myself happy in spite of everything. I felt as if I had just received a wonderful part. I was so strong. But I didn't notice the street car. Fortunately I jumped back in time. I was scared, my heart was palpitating, but I still remembered "the happiness of my existence". So I smiled at the motorman and ordered him to proceed. He said something to me, but I couldn't understand him—he was talking behind the glass.

I: I suspect it was just as well that you didn't distinguish his words.

THE CREATURE: Oh, I see. And do you think he was right—being rude to me?

I: I could justify him. You destroyed his concentration as thoroughly as he destroyed yours. That is

30

where the drama began. The result was—action expressed in his words behind the glass and in your command to proceed.

THE CREATURE: Oh, you make fun of everything.

I: No, I don't. I think yours is a case of drama in a nutshell. Active drama.

THE CREATURE: Do you mean to say that it helped my ability to act? My sense of drama?

I: Yes, I do.

THE CREATURE: How?

I: It will take some time to explain. Won't you sit down and first tell me why you came to me today? Is it another *King Lear?*

THE CREATURE: Oh, please! *(Blush—powder on the nose—hat off—hair adjusted. She sits down; another dab of powder on the nose.)*

I: *(As kind as my cigar permits me to be)* You needn't be ashamed of anything, especially of that *King Lear* performance. You were sincere then. That was a year ago; you wanted a little bit too much but you went after it in the right way. You just did it. You made the attack yourself. You didn't wait for somebody to push you. You know the story of the fair-haired school boy who had to walk a long way to school. Every day for years he said to himself, "Oh, if I could only fly, I could get to school so much quicker." Well, you know what happened to him.

THE CREATURE: No.

31

I: He flew from New York to Paris, alone—his name was Lindbergh. He is a colonel now.

THE CREATURE: Yes. *(A pause)* Can I talk to you seriously? *(She is dreaming now; she has learned to make good use of everything that comes to her. Inward or outward, she doesn't miss the slightest hint of emotion. She is like a violin whose strings respond to all vibrations, and she remembers those vibrations. I am sure she takes all there is in life as only a strong, normal being can take it. She selects what she wants to keep; she throws away what seems worthless to her. She will make a good actress.)*

I: Yes, but not solemnly.

THE CREATURE: I am going to talk to you about myself. *(She smiles.)* And . . . *(Lugubriously)* My Art.

I: I hate the way you say, "My art." Why do you become so serious when you say it? You smile at yourself. Only a few minutes ago you told me that your only reason for living must be "the *happiness* of your existence". Why do people get solemn as soon as they speak of things which have no purpose but to bring joy to others!

THE CREATURE: I don't know about other people, but I am serious because art means everything to me. That is why I came here again, because I simply must make good. I have been given a part and have rehearsed for four days. I feel that I'm not very secure in it. Three days more and they may take it away from me. They say pleasant things to me, but I know I am not right—and nobody seems to know how to help me. They say, "speak louder", "feel something", "pick up your cues", "laugh", "sob", and what not, but I know that isn't all. There must be something missing. What is it? Where? Where am I to get it? I have done everything you told me to do. I think I control myself—that is, my body, very well. I've practised for a whole year. The body positions that the part demands are not difficult for me. I feel comfortable in all of them. I use my five senses simply and logically. I am happy when I act and still I don't know how! I don't know how! What shall I do? If they fire me, it will be the end of me. And the worst of it all is that I know only too well what they will all say. They will say, "You are very good, but you lack experience"—and that's all. What is that cursed experience? There isn't a thing anybody can tell me about that part—I know everything about it. I look like it, I feel every single minute of it and each change. I know I can act it. And then—"experience"! Oh, I wish I could use some of the words that that motorman used who nearly ran over me. I didn't hear them, but judging from his face, I know they would be right. As a matter of fact, I think I can guess what they were—and oh, how I could use them now!

I: Go ahead and use them. Don't mind me. (*She uses them.*) Any happier?

THE CREATURE: Yes. (*Smile. Laugh.*)

33

I: All right, now you are ready. Now I'll talk to you. Let's talk about your part. You will work it out for yourself, and what's more, you'll do it right. If you have done all the work you say you have and if the part is within your range, you cannot fail. Don't worry about it. Work and patience never fail.

THE CREATURE: Oh, teacher . . . *(She starts.)*

I: Sit down. I mean it. For a year you have been perfecting yourself as a human instrument and gathering material. You have observed and absorbed life. You have collected what you saw, read, heard and felt in the storage places of your brain. You did it both consciously and unconsciously. Concentration became your second nature.

THE CREATURE: I don't think I did anything unconsciously. I am a very matter-of-fact person.

I: I know you are. The actor must be—how otherwise could he dream? The only person who can dream is the person who can stand with both feet firmly on the earth. That is why the Irish policeman is the best policeman in the world. He never sleeps on duty. He dreams wide awake. And the gangster has little chance.

THE CREATURE: Please! I have a part. I want to act it and you talk about Irish policemen.

I: No, I am talking about the practicality of dreams. I'm talking about order, about system. I'm talking about harnessing dreams—conscious and unconscious

34

dreams—all useful—all necessary—all obedient—all coming at your call. All parts in that beautiful state of your nature that you call "experience".

THE CREATURE: All right. But what about my part?

I: You will have to organize and synchronize the self that is within you, with your part. Then everything will be splendid.

THE CREATURE: All right, let's start.

I: First of all, I insist—and you will have to believe me—that you did a great deal of your work unconsciously. Now we'll start. What is the most important scene in your part?

THE CREATURE: The scene where I tell my mother that I'm going to leave her house, her poor and obscure house, for an extraordinary reason. A rich lady has become interested in me and is going to take me into her home to give me all the beautiful things of life—education, travel, friends, beautiful surroundings, clothes, jewels, position—everything. It's too marvelous. I cannot withstand temptation. I must go, but I love my mother and am sorry for her. I struggle between the lure of happiness and love for my mother. My decision is not yet made, but the desire for happiness is very strong.

I: Good. Now, how will you do it, and what does your director say?

THE CREATURE: He says that I am either happy

35

to go away or love my mother so much that I am not at all happy to go. I cannot blend these two things.

I: You must be happy and sorry at the same time. Gleaming and tender.

THE CREATURE: That's it. I can't feel those two things simultaneously.

I: Nobody can, but you can *be* that.

THE CREATURE: To *be* that without feeling it? How is that possible?

I: With the help of your unconscious memory—of your memory of feelings.

THE CREATURE: Unconscious memory of feelings? You mean to say that I must unconsciously memorize my feelings?

I: God forbid. We have a special memory for feelings, which works unconsciously by itself and for itself. It's right there. It is in every artist. It is that which makes experience an essential part of our life and craft. All we have to do is to know how to use it.

THE CREATURE: But where is it? How do you get it? Does anybody know about it?

I: Oh, quite a number of people. The French psychologist, Théodule Ribot,* was the first to speak of it over twenty years ago. He calls it "affective memory" or "memory of affects."

THE CREATURE: How does it work?

* Théodule Ribot: *Problèmes de Psychologie Affective:* Felix Actan. Paris.

36

I: Through all the manifestations of life and our sensitivity toward them.

THE CREATURE: For example?

I: For example, in a certain city there lived a couple who had been married for twenty-five years. They had married when they were very young. He had proposed to her one fine summer evening when they were walking in a cucumber patch. Being nervous, as nice young people are apt to be under the circumstances, they would stop occasionally, pick a cucumber and eat it, enjoying very much its aroma, taste and the freshness and richness of the sun's warmth upon it. They made the happiest decision of their lives, between two mouthfuls of cucumbers, so to speak.

A month later they were married. At the wedding supper a dish of fresh cucumbers was served—and nobody knew why they laughed so heartily when they saw it. Long years of life and struggle came; children and, naturally, difficulties. Sometimes they quarreled, and were angry. Sometimes they did not even speak to each other. But their youngest daughter observed that the surest way to make peace between them was to put a dish of cucumbers on the table. Like magic they would forget their quarrels, and would become tender and understanding. For a long time the daughter thought the change was due to their love for cucumbers, but once the mother told her the story of

37

their courtship, and when she thought about it, she came to another conclusion. I wonder if you can?

THE CREATURE: *(Very brightly)* Yes, the outward circumstances brought back the inward feelings.

I: I wouldn't say feelings. I would say rather, made these two people what they were long years before, in spite of time, reason, and maybe—desire, *unconsciously*.

THE CREATURE: No, not unconsciously, because they knew what the cucumbers had meant to them.

I: After twenty-five years? I doubt it. They were simple souls, they wouldn't go so far as to analyze the origin of their feelings. They just naturally yielded themselves to the feelings as they came. They were stronger than any present feeling. It is just as when you start to count, "One, two, three, four," it takes an effort not to continue, "five, six, etc." The whole thing is to make a beginning—to start.

THE CREATURE: Do you think I have . . . ?

I: Undoubtedly.

THE CREATURE: I wanted to ask if you thought I had memories like that in me.

I: Plenty of them—just waiting to be awakened, just waiting for a call. And what is more, when you do awaken them, you can control them, you can make use of them, you can apply them in your craft. I prefer that word to the word "Art" which you like so much. You can learn the whole secret of experience.

38

THE CREATURE: But not stage experience.

I: Indirectly, yes. Because when you have something to say, the experience comes so much more quickly, a hundred times faster than when you have nothing to say. It comes much more surely than when all you do is to *try* to be experienced, to "speak louder", to "feel something", to "pick up the cues", to "hold the tempo." Those are problems for children, not for craftsmen.

THE CREATURE: But how do you go about those things? How do you command them?

I: That's the spirit. You *command* them. In your particular case did you or did you not ever experience that double feeling when you are sad and happy at the same time?

THE CREATURE: Yes, yes, many times, but I don't know how to bring it back. I don't *remember* where I was and what I was doing when I felt that way.

I: Never mind where and what. The point is to bring yourself back as you were then, to command your own ego, go where you want to go, and when you are there, to stay where you went. Give me an example of your personal experience with a double feeling.

THE CREATURE: Well, I went abroad last summer for the first time in my life. My brother couldn't go. He saw me off. I was happy and at the same time I was sorry for him. But how I acted I don't remember.

39

## THE SECOND LESSON

I: All right. Tell me how the whole thing happened. Start at the moment you left your house. Don't omit any details. Give me a description of the taxi driver and of all your worries and excitements. Try to recall the weather, the color of the sky, the smells at the docks, the voices of longshoremen and sailors, the faces of fellow-passengers. Give me a good journalistic account of the whole thing and forget about yourself. Work outwardly. Start with your clothing and that of your brother. Go on.

*(She starts. Well trained in concentration, she throws herself into the subject. She could give a lesson to any detective. She is cold, firm, exact, analytical—not missing details, not using meaningless words—giving only necessary bare facts. At first she is almost mechanical, almost a perfect machine. Then when she speaks of a traffic officer who stops the taxi and reads a sermon to the driver, and she exclaims, "Oh, please, Officer, we will be late," the first sign of real emotion comes into her eyes. She starts to be—she starts to act. It does not come easily. Seven times she goes back to facts and only facts, but gradually they are of less and less importance. When she finally tells how she ran up the gangway and jumped on to the deck of the steamer, her face and eyes are shining, involuntarily she repeats the jump. Then suddenly she turns her face, and there, not far away, is her brother down on the pier. Tears come to her eyes. She conceals them. "Cheer up, cheer up," she cries. "I'll tell you all about*

40

*it. Give my love to everybody. Oh, how I hate to leave New York. I'd rather stay with you, but it's too late now. Besides you wouldn't want me to. Oh, it's going to be too wonderful . . .")*

I: Stop. Now go on with the speech from your part in the play. Don't lose what you've got. Just exactly as you are now—speaking to your brother. You are what you ought to be in the part.

THE CREATURE: But I am speaking to my mother in the part.

I: Is she really your mother?

THE CREATURE: No.

I: Then what difference does it make? The theatre exists to show things which do not exist actually. When you love on the stage, do you really love? Be logical. You substitute creation for the real thing. The creation must be real, but that is the only reality that should be there. Your experience of double feeling was a fortunate accident. Through your will-power and the knowledge of your craft you have organized it and re-created it. It is now in your hands. Use it if your artistic sense tells you that it is relative to your problem and creates a would-be life. To imitate is wrong. To create is right.

THE CREATURE: But while you were speaking, I lost what seemed to be that very important process of re-creation. Do I have to begin my story again? Must I go back again to that state of double feeling?

I: How do you learn a tune you want to remember?

How do you learn the outline of muscles you want to draw? How do you learn the mixture of colors you want to use in painting? Through constant repetition and perfection. It may be hard for you, easier for someone else.

One person remembers a tune, hearing it just once —another will have to hear it many times. Toscanini remembers it, reading a manuscript once. Practice! I have given you an example. You can find around and within you hundreds of opportunities. Work on them and learn to bring back what seems lost. Learn to bring it back actually and make good use of it. At first it will require much time, skill, and effort. The subject is delicate. You will find the trend and lose it again many times. Don't get discouraged. Remember, this is an actor's fundamental work—to be able "to be" what he desires consciously and exactly.

THE CREATURE: In my particular case, how would you suggest that I bring back what I seem to have found and lost?

I: First of all, work on it alone. It was all right for me to demonstrate as I did to show you the way, but your actual work is done in solitude—entirely inside of yourself. You know how, now, through concentration. Think over the process of approach toward the actual moment of that real double feeling. You will know when you get it. You will feel the warmth of it and the satisfaction.

42

Practically every good actor does it unconsciously when he acts well and is happy about it. However, gradually, it will take you less and less time. It will be just like recalling a tune. Finally the flash of thought will be sufficient. You will eliminate details. You will define the whole thing inside of your being with certain aim, and with practice, a mere hint will make you "be" what you want. Then use the author's words and if your choice was right, they will always sound fresh, always alive! You won't need to play them. You'll hardly need to form them, they will come so naturally. All you will need is to have perfect bodily technique in order to project whatever emotion you are prompted to express.

THE CREATURE: And if the choice of my own feelings is not right, what then?

I: Have you seen a manuscript of Wagner's music? If you are in Bayreuth, go to see one. See how many times Wagner erased and crossed out notes and melodies and harmonies until he found the one he wanted. If he did it so many times, surely you can try no less often.

THE CREATURE: Suppose I don't find a similar feeling in my life's experience, what then?

I: Impossible! If you are a sensitive and normal human being, all life is open and familiar to you. After all, poets and playwrights are human too. If they find experience in their lives to use, why shouldn't you? But you will have to use your imagination; you can never tell where you will find the thing you are after.

THE CREATURE: All right, suppose I have to play murder. I have never murdered anybody. How shall I find it?

I: Oh, why do actors always ask me about murder? The younger they are the more murders they want to act. All right, you have never murdered anybody. Have you ever camped?

THE CREATURE: Yes.

I: Ever sat in the woods at the edge of a lake after sundown?

THE CREATURE: Yes.

I: Were there any mosquitoes around?

THE CREATURE: It was in New Jersey.

I: Did they annoy you? Did you follow one among them with your eyes and ears and hate until the beast landed on your forearm? And did you slap your forearm cruelly without even thinking of the hurt to yourself—with only the wish to . . . end?

THE CREATURE: *(Quite ashamed)* To kill the beast.

I: There you are. A good sensitive artist doesn't need any more than that to play Othello and Desdemona's final scene. The rest is the work of magnification, imagination, and belief.

Gordon Craig has a charming book-plate, fantastic,

44

with an unusual, beautiful pattern—unknown and strange. You cannot tell what it is, but it gives you a sense of brooding, a sense of boring through, a sense of slow drive and struggle. It is nothing but a book-worm, a common book-worm, enlarged many times. An artist will find his source anywhere. Nature has not given one-hundredth part of what it still holds for you. Go and look for it. One of the most charming grotesque actors on the stage is Ed Wynn. Can you see where he began his trick of putting a windshield with a wiper before his eyes when he started to eat a grapefruit? Can't you see how he watched the mud and the water as he drove along in his car, protected by the real windshield, watched it with perfect satisfaction, feeling safe? Then, once at luncheon, perhaps, he got an eyeful of grapefruit juice. He associated the two ideas, and the result—a charming foolery.

THE CREATURE: I doubt that he thought it out that way.

I: Certainly not. But unconsciously he went through the whole process. How do you expect to learn your craft if you don't analyze what has been already achieved? Then forget about it all and go after your own achievements.

THE CREATURE: What do you do when you find places in the part where you cannot apply that "to be" of yours?

I: You must find it for every place, but be careful

45

not to overdo it. Don't look for "to be" when you should seek "to do." Don't forget that when you want to be an actor with all your heart and soul, want it to such an extent that you forget your self entirely, and when your technique is developed sufficiently, you can already act most of the stuff that is written. It is just like humming a tune. The difficult spots are what you should watch for and work for. Every play is written for one or at most a few "high tension" moments. The audience pays the price of the tickets—not for two whole hours—but for the best ten seconds, the ten seconds when it gets the biggest laugh or thrill. Your whole strength and perfection must be directed toward those seconds.

THE CREATURE: Thanks, I have them in my part. I know now what was wrong—there are three places which I haven't lifted above the rest of the play— that is why I was monotonous. I will look forward now "to be" in those places. Are you sure they will come out all right?

I: Sure as I am that you will soon come back to me with another problem.

THE CREATURE: Oh, I was so foolish not to come back to you right away.

I: Not at all. It takes at least a year to get the foundation for your technique. You've got enough to be an actress now. So nothing is lost. If I had told you a year ago what I am telling you now, you wouldn't have understood it, and you would never have come back. Now you have come and something tells me your next visit will be quite soon. I think I even know when—when you get a part which won't be yourself—where you will have to change yourself a little bit—where you will no longer be a mere convenient type, but must become a daring artist.

THE CREATURE: May I come tomorrow?

I: No, not until you act your part. I hope you will act it very well. And I hope you won't get very good notices. Nothing is so bad for a young artist as glorifying notices. When that happens, before you realize it, you become lazy and are late for rehearsals.

THE CREATURE: That reminds me.

I: I know. That's why I said it. Go and rehearse now. As happy and as strong as ever. You have something beautiful to work on. Meantime, remember that little story about cucumbers.

Notice everything around you—watch yourself cheerfully. Collect and save in your soul all the riches of life and the fulness of it. Keep those memories in order. You can never tell when you will need them, but they are your only friends and teachers in your craft. They are your only paints and brushes. And they will bring you reward. They are yours—your own property. They are not imitations, and they will give you experience, precision, economy, and power.

THE CREATURE: Yes. Thanks.

47

I: And the next time you come to me, bring me at least a hundred records of your registered moments when you made yourself "to be" what you wanted when you wanted.

THE CREATURE: Oh, don't you worry. The next time I come to you I will know my . . . cucumbers.

*(She goes away, strong, alive, and beautiful; I am left alone with my cigar.)*

I wonder who said, "The object of Education is not to know but to live."

# THE THIRD LESSON

## *Dramatic Action*

The Creature and I are walking in the park. She is in a rage. She has been rehearsing a part in the talkies.

THE CREATURE: . . . and then they stopped. I waited for an hour and a half. We started. This time three lines from the big scene; three lines—that was all. After that again a wait of an hour. It is impossible —simply impossible. Machinery, electricity, lenses, microphone, furniture, that is all that counts. An actor? Who cares? Acting? A miserable accessory.

I: And yet a few actors achieve quite a high degree of dramatic art.

THE CREATURE: Now and then—for five seconds—rare as black pearls.

I: If you look for them, not so rare.

THE CREATURE: Oh, how can you say so? You, who all your life advocated the magnificent, flowing, live theatre. How can you look for rare moments of beauty in talkies? Even when you find them they are separated, disjointed, cut, uneven. How can you defend those moments and justify them?

I: Tell me, have I helped you before with my talks?

THE CREATURE: You have.

I: Are you willing to listen now, with as little interruption as possible?

THE CREATURE: I am.

I: All right. Look at that marble fountain. It was made in 1902 by Arthur Collins.

THE CREATURE: How do you know?

I: It is chiselled on the rim of the base. You promised not to interrupt me.

THE CREATURE: Sorry.

I: How do you like Mr. Collins' work?

THE CREATURE: Not bad. Quite simple and clear in form. It harmonizes with the landscape; it is noble. Made in 1902, it has definite traces of modern conception. What else has Arthur Collins done?

I: This is the last work he ever did. He died—35 years of age. He was a promising sculptor. Though young, he influenced many of the modern masters.

THE CREATURE: I can see it. Isn't it wonderful that he left his work behind him so that we can look at it, trace the line of creative descent, and understand the vision of our contemporaries.

I: It is wonderful, indeed. Wouldn't you like to see and hear Mrs. Siddons right now, acting the lines:

> "Here's the smell of the blood still; all
> the perfumes of Arabia will not sweeten this
> little hand. Oh! Oh! Oh!"

What would you give to learn what Mrs. Siddons did with those "Oh! Oh! Oh!'s"? They say that people used to faint when she did it; we don't know. And wouldn't you like to hear David Garrick, in *Richard III*, scorn William Catesby:

> "Slave! I have set my life upon a cast.
> And I will stand the hazard of the die."

Or Jefferson, or Booth, or Ellen Terry? I still remember Salvini's reaction when Iago would say:

> "But he that filches from me my good name
> Robs me of that which not enriches him,
> And makes me poor indeed."

I tried once to describe it. In vain. It is gone. This fountain speaks for itself. There is nothing to speak for Salvini.

THE CREATURE: Really, it is a pity . . . *(She pauses, grows pensive and then says, with a wistful smile—)* Well, it seems that I gave you a cue.

I: You always give me the cues. I don't invent things. I observe them and present them to you; you draw the conclusions and profit by them. The only real rules in art are the rules that we discover for ourselves.

THE CREATURE: I have discovered that it is too bad not to have the images and voices of great actors preserved for posterity. Now, I'm drawing a conclusion; because of that I must suffer in my work the mechanism and cheapness of the talkies?

I: No. The only thing you have to do is to march abreast of your times, and do your best—as an artist.

THE CREATURE: Impossible.

I: Inevitable.

THE CREATURE: It is a false vogue—a fad.

I: Narrow way of thinking.

THE CREATURE: My whole nature as an actress rebels against that mechanical monster.

I: Then you are not an actress.

THE CREATURE: Because I want a free, uninterrupted outlet for my inspiration and creative work?

I: No. Because you do not rejoice in the discovery of a great and final instrument of drama; the instrument which all the other arts have had since time immemorial, and which the oldest art, the theatre, lacked until today; the instrument that gives to the theatre the precision and scientific serenity which all the other arts have had; the instrument that demands of the actor to be as exact as the color scheme in painting, form in sculpture, string, wood, brass in music, mathematics in architecture, words in poetry.

THE CREATURE: But look at the hundreds of incredibly stupid talkies appearing each week—poor acting, insignificant action, wrong rhythm.

I: Look at the hundreds of millions of stupid paintings, songs, performances, houses and books that have appeared since the beginning of time, that have gone into oblivion without hurting anybody while the good ones survived.

THE CREATURE: Is one good talkie worth hundreds of bad ones?

I: Be generous. The idea is worth them. It is the preservation of the art of the actor—the art of the theatre. Spoken drama equally with written drama. Do you realize that with the invention of spontaneous recording of the image, movement and voice, and consequently the personality and soul of an actor, the last missing link in the chain of the arts disappears, and the theatre is no more a passing affair, but an eternal record? Do you realize that the intimate creative work of an actor need no longer be performed before the public eye; that there need be no more dragging the audience into a sweat and labor over your work? The

53

actor is free from onlookers in the moment of creation and only the results of it are judged.

THE CREATURE: The actor in front of machinery is not free. He is chopped to pieces—almost every sentence of his part is separated from the previous and the following ones.

I: Every word of a poet is separated from the other words. The assembled whole is what counts.

THE CREATURE: But how can one get the flow of the part? How can one build up an emotion and rise to the unconscious climaxes of real inspired interpretation of a part?

I: In the way one should do it in the theatre. Because you have had one or two successful parts on the stage you think there is nothing more to learn, nothing more to improve or to build up in your technique.

THE CREATURE: You know that isn't so. I always want to learn. Otherwise I wouldn't be walking with you for the second time around this silly lake.

I: Well, our walk is smooth, continuous, easy flowing, building up toward a climax.

THE CREATURE: Which will be when I drop breathless on the grass?

I: Exactly, and that's the way you play your parts—rushing through them, building up emotion and chasing the climax until you drop in a critic's lap trying to catch a breath. And you don't get much breath from them either.

54

THE CREATURE: Well, I can see that something is coming. What is it?

I: What was your main difficulty acting in the talkies?

THE CREATURE: Lack of springboard. Being compelled to start a scene in the middle and finish it after four or five lines, then in another hour start another scene (which in the script comes before the previous one), then again act four lines and wait an hour. I tell you it's abnormal, it's horrible—

I: Lack of technique, that's all.

THE CREATURE: What technique?

I: Of action's structure.

THE CREATURE: Stage action?

I: Dramatic action which the writer expresses in words, having that action as the purpose and goal of his words, and which the actor performs, or acts, as the word actor itself implies.

THE CREATURE: That is exactly what it is impossible to do in the talkies. I had a love scene, two and a half pages in the script, and when I was acting it I was interrupted eleven times. It took the whole day. My action was to convince the man who loved me that I loved him too, but was terrified by his father's hatred of me.

I: This on two and a half pages?—you said it in one line, quite convincingly. What did you do for the remainder of the two and a half pages?

THE CREATURE: I tried to do the same thing.

I: For two and a half pages? Thank God they did interrupt you eleven times.

THE CREATURE: That was the action. What else was there to do?

I: Look at that tree. It is the protagonist of all arts; it is an ideal structure of action. Upward movement and sideway resistance, balance and growth.

THE CREATURE: Granted.

I: Look at the trunk—straight, proportioned, harmonious with the rest of the tree, supporting every part of it. It is the leading strain; "Leitmotif" in music; a director's idea of action in a play; the architect's foundation; the poet's thought in a sonnet.

THE CREATURE: How does a director express that action in producing a play?

I: Through interpretation of the play, and through ingenious combinations of smaller, secondary, or complementary actions that will secure that interpretation.

THE CREATURE: Give an example.

I: All right. *The Taming of the Shrew* is a play where two people long to love each other in spite of their impossible characters, and succeed in their longing. It might also be a play about a man who triumphs over a woman by "treating her rough". It might be a play about a woman who makes everybody's life miserable. Do you grasp the difference?

THE CREATURE: I do.

I: In the first case the action is to love; in the second swash-buckling; in the third the anger of a vixen.

THE CREATURE: Do you mean to say that in the first case, for instance, when the action is love, you would make the actors assume the attitude of love all the way through?

I: I would make them remember it. I would ask them to have it behind every curse, every quarrel, every disagreement.

THE CREATURE: What would you expect from an actor?

I: To comply with nature's law of action, the threefold law you can see expressed in that tree. First, the main trunk, the idea, the reason. On the stage it comes from the director. Second, the branches, elements of the idea, particles of reason. That comes from the actor. Third, the foliage, the result of the previous two, the brilliant presentation of idea, the bright conclusion of reasoning.

THE CREATURE: Where does the author appear on the scene?

I: He is the sap that flows and feeds the whole.

THE CREATURE: *(With a twinkle in her eyes)* That was a narrow escape for the actor.

I: *(With a twinkle in my eyes also)* Well, if he doesn't know how to project his actions in front of . . .

57

THE CREATURE: That's enough. I take it on the chin.

I: . . . the camera and microphone, and is afraid of eleven interruptions. . . .

THE CREATURE: *(She stops and stamps her foot.)* All right. All right. *(She is very much annoyed.)* Tell me how *not* to be afraid of them.

I: I need a written part or a play to show you exactly what I mean by the structure of action. I haven't one with me.

THE CREATURE: We have acted a nice little play right through, during our walk in the last half hour. Whenever we talk, we always do, as a matter of fact. Why don't you use what we have talked over as a play?

I: All right. I'm the director. You are a young actress performing a one-act play with a grumpy old man. I am that man, also.

THE CREATURE: Let's talk about characterizations later, another time.

I: At your service. Now the director is speaking: The trunk, or the "spine" of your little play, my friends (meaning you and me), is the discovery of truth about dramatic action, not on a dark stage, or in a classroom, or from learned books, or in front of an angry director ready to fire you, but in the midst of nature, enjoying air, sun, a brisk walk and good humor.

THE CREATURE: Which means quick thinking, energetic penetration, bright spirit, conviction in ideas, eagerness to understand, clear voices, fast tempo, and readiness to argue, to give and to take.

I: Bravo! Bravo! As the director I'm through. With your help we have established the trunk or "spine". Now, let's turn to the sap.

THE CREATURE: Meaning the author . . . ?

I: Exactly. Is that nice?

THE CREATURE: *(Runs away from me, claps her hands and laughs with the most childish satisfaction. I run after her, and catch her by the hand.)*

I: We are even. Let's continue, and analyze the words in terms of action. Let's take your part. What did you do at the beginning of the play?

THE CREATURE: I complained . . .

I: . . . Bitterly and exaggeratedly . . .

THE CREATURE: . . . I scorned and despised . . .

I: . . . With the charming resolution of youth.

THE CREATURE: . . . I piled up the evidence.

I: Not convincingly, but forcefully.

THE CREATURE: I didn't believe you . . . and reproached you.

I: Like a stubborn youngster. And you have forgotten that at the same time you walked, sometimes you agreed with me, you observed and studied Mr. Collins' fountain, you felt physically tired, you looked for words to oppose my arguments, you enjoyed a few

59

Shakespearean lines, and with all that you covered about nine speeches.

THE CREATURE: *(Horrified)* Have I done all those things at once?

I: Never. No human being could. But having the main trunk, or thread of action in mind, what you did was to string on that thread the secondary, or complementary actions like beads on a string, one after another, sometimes overlapping each other but always clear and distinct.

THE CREATURE: Weren't they just intonations and inflections?

I: Where would they come from, if not as the result of action?

THE CREATURE: That's true.

I: Describing your actions, you used only verbs— that is significant. A verb is action in itself. First you want something, it is your artist's will; then you define it in a verb, it is your artist's technique; and then you actually do it, it is your artist's expression. You do it through the medium of speech—words of a . . .

THE CREATURE: My own words in this case.

I: It doesn't matter, although some clever author's words would have been much better.

THE CREATURE: *(Nods silently—it is so hard to agree while one is young.)*

I: The author would have written them for you. Then you could take a pencil and write "music of action" under every word or speech, as you write music to lyrics for a song; then on the stage you would play that "music of action". You would have to memorize your actions as you memorize the music. You would have to know distinctly the difference between "I complained" and "I scorned" and, although the two actions follow each other, you would be just as different in their delivery as the singer is when he takes "C" or "C flat".

Moreover, when you know action by heart no interruption or change of order can disturb you. If you have your action confined within one single word, and you know exactly what that action is, you have it inside of you on the call of a split second, how can you be disturbed when the time comes for its delivery? Your scene, or part, is a long string of beads—beads of action. You play with them as you play with a rosary. You can start anywhere, any time, and go as far as you wish, if you have a good hold on the beads themselves.

THE CREATURE: But doesn't it happen that the same action may last for pages, or at least a very long scene?

I: Certainly, only it is more difficult for the actor to keep it going without monotony—"To be or not to be" has nine sentences with one single action . . .

THE CREATURE: What is it?

I: To be or not to be. Shakespeare did not take

any chances with actors. He told them right in the beginning what he wanted them to do. On account of the significance of that action and the length of the scene itself it is the hardest thing to act. To recite it is very easy.

THE CREATURE: I understand. The recitation is like the foliage of a tree without the trunk and branches.

I: Precisely—just juggling with the modulation of voice and artificial pauses. Even in the best case with a very well trained voice it is only poor music. As drama, it is nil.

THE CREATURE: What was your action when you started to enumerate the names of actors and speeches in their parts? You really looked sorrowful and wistful. Have you forgotten the agreed "spine"? We decided it must be "energy, bright spirit, quick thinking" and so on. . . .

I: No. But what I wanted was to make you say, "It is a pity." I could do it in one way only, namely by arousing your sympathy toward my feelings. That in turn made you think about my words, and you yourself drew the conclusion that I was looking for.

THE CREATURE: In other words, you acted sorrowful to make me pensive?

I: Yes, and I acted it "energetically, with bright spirit and quick thinking."

THE CREATURE: Could you perform some other action with the same words, and get the same results?

I: Yes. But my action was prompted by you.

THE CREATURE: By me?

I: Yes. By your character rather. To convince you in anything one must approach you through emotion. Cold reasoning is inaccessible to your type of mind— the mind of an artist who deals mostly with his or other people's imaginations. If, instead of you, I had had a bearded Professor of History as a companion, I wouldn't have acted sorrowful at all. I would have tempted him enthusiastically with a picture of the past —a weak spot of all historians—and he would have yielded to my statement.

THE CREATURE: I see. So one must choose his actions in accordance with the character of the part that opposes him.

I: Always. Not only the character of the part, but also the individuality of the actor who plays the part.

THE CREATURE: How do I memorize the action?

I: After you have found the feeling through your "memory of affects". You remember our last talk?

THE CREATURE: I do.

I: You are ready for action. Rehearsals serve the purpose. You repeat the action a few times and you remember it. Actions are very easy to remember— much easier than words. Tell me right now, what did you act in the first nine speeches of our play—the one we went through?

THE CREATURE: (*Bursts into rapid energetic enu-*

*meration. All her heart is in it.)* I complained, scorned, despised. I reproached you. I didn't believe you. . . .

I: And what is your action now, while you are enthusiastically throwing all those hateful verbs into my face?

THE CREATURE: I . . . I . . .

I: Come on—what is your action?

THE CREATURE: I am proving to you that I believe your words.

I: And I believe you, because you have proved it with action.

# THE FOURTH LESSON

## *Characterization*

I am waiting for the Creature at the stage entrance. She is with a company in an important play. She has asked me to come after rehearsal and take her home. She wants to talk to me about her part.

I do not have long to wait. The door opens. She comes out hurriedly. Tired, her eyes gleaming, her lovely hair dishevelled, a tender flush of excitement on her cheeks.

THE CREATURE: I'm sorry to disappoint you. I cannot go with you. I'm not going home. I have to stay here and rehearse.

I: I saw all the actors leaving—Are you going to rehearse alone?

THE CREATURE: *(Nodding sadly)* Uh-mmmm—

I: Any trouble?

THE CREATURE: Plenty.

I: May I come in and watch you rehearse?

THE CREATURE: Thank you. I was afraid to ask you.

I: Why?

THE CREATURE: *(Lifts herself on her toes and whispers into my ear, her eyes round with horror—)* I'm very, Oh, very, bad.

I: I would rather hear you say that than 'Come and see me—I'm very, Oh, very good.'

THE CREATURE: Well, I'm saying that I'm bad because it's all your fault. In this new part I have done everything you told me, and still I'm bad.

I: All right, let's see.

*(We pass a very old doorman in his shirt sleeves, smoking a pipe. He looks at me with deep-set, dark eyes from under bushy eyebrows. His clean-shaven face is set firmly. He is not letting anybody in. His very presence bars the entrance. He acts the part. He is not just a watchman—he is a splendid impersonation of Francisco, Bernardo, or Marcellus at his post. He raises his hand in a noble gesture.)*

THE CREATURE: That's all right, Pa, the gentleman is with me.

66

# CHARACTERIZATION

*(The old man nods silently, and in his old eyes I can read permission to enter. I think to myself 'It takes an actor to be so economically gracious. I wonder if he is one?' I take my hat off as I enter the stage. It is dark. One electric bulb etches a halo in the centre of the darkness. The Creature takes me by the hand and leads me down the stairway and among the stalls into the pit.)*

THE CREATURE: Sit here, please; don't say anything; don't interrupt me. Let me act a few scenes in succession for you, then tell me what is wrong.

*(She goes back to the stage. I am left alone, in a space bordered by glittering dark holes of boxes, by silent rows of chairs covered with canvas, by faint outside noises. All the shadows are strange and solid. The quiet is trembling and alive. I respond to that quiet. My nerves begin to vibrate and to throw threads of sympathy and expectation toward the great promising black riddle, the empty stage. A peculiar peace descends on my mind, as if I partially cease to exist and somebody else's soul is living in me instead of my own. I will be dead to myself, alive to the outward world. I will observe and participate in an imaginary world. I will wake up with my heart full of dreams. Sweet poison of an empty theatre, empty stage and a single actor rehearsing on it.*

*The Creature appears. She has a book in her hand. She tries to read, but her mind is distracted. Obviously*

*she is waiting for somebody. It must be somebody of
importance indeed. She seems to tremble. She looks
around as if asking approval and advice from an invisible friend. She is encouraged; I can hear her faint
sigh.*

*Then suddenly she sees somebody in the far dis-
tance. She stiffens, draws her breath quickly. She must
be afraid. She makes as if to read from the book. But
it is clear to me that she does not see a single letter.
Not a word is spoken. I am watching tensely and
whisper to myself 'Well done, well done, Creature,
I'm ready now for every word you utter.'*

*The Creature listens. Her body is relaxed, the hand
holding the book hangs limply. Her head is turned
slightly to one side, an unconscious help to the ear
through which imaginary words enter her soul. She
nods her head.)*

THE CREATURE:

"Good my lord,
How does your honour for this many a day?"

*(There is a warm, sincere affection and respect in
her voice. She speaks as if to an elder brother. Then
she looks, with fear and trembling, for an imaginary
answer. The answer comes.)*

· · · · · ·

*(She closes her eyes for a moment.)*
"My lord, I have remembrances of yours,
  That I have longed long to re-deliver;
  I pray you, now receive them."

68

*(What is it? She sounds as if she were not telling quite the truth. Expectant fear in her voice. She stands as if petrified. She looks around again as if for the support of an invisible friend. Suddenly she shrinks back as if hit by the imaginary answer.)*

. . . . . .

*(It must have been a blow, right at the heart. Her book falls, her trembling fingers clutch one another. She defends herself.)*

"My honour'd lord, you know right well you did;
  And, with them, words of so sweet breath compos'd
  As made the things more rich: their perfume lost,
  Take these again; for to the noble mind
  Rich gifts wax poor when givers prove unkind."

*(Her voice breaks, then suddenly soars freely and strongly in defense of injured pride and love.)*

"There, my lord."

*(She seems to grow taller. It is the result of co-ordination between her muscles and her emotion, the first sign of a trained actress: the stronger the emotion, the more freedom in the voice, the more relaxation in muscles.)*

. . . . . .

"My lord?"

*(There is an almost masculine strength in that fragile body.)*

. . . . . .

"What means your lordship?"

*(Her fear forgotten, she speaks now as an equal.*

69

*She does not look around for help or confirmation of her actions. She throws the words into the black space without seeming to wait for an answer.)*

. . . . . .

"Could beauty, my lord, have better commerce than
with honesty?"

. . . . . .

*(Then a change comes over her face. Pain, tenderness, sorrow, adoration, all are in her eyes and on her trembling lips. I understand; the enemy is the beloved one. A whispered line—like moaning wind—)*
"Indeed, my lord, you made me believe so."

. . . . . .

*(And still more quietly and sorrowfully)*
"I was the more deceived."

. . . . . .

*(Then comes a long silence. She absorbs inaudible words of anger, shame, accusation, words which throw her to earth and remind her of somebody whom she has forgotten in her sincerity but who has power over her and who has told her exactly what to do. She is conscious of him now. She is not herself, she is an obedient daughter. She is a tool in her father's hands. Suddenly she shudders. She hears the inevitable question, the compromising question. And again a lie is the answer, a torturing lie.)*
"At home, my lord."

. . . . . .

70

# CHARACTERIZATION

*(Horror lashes her; despair makes her sob from the depths of her soul, as if all her being wailed, Oh, what have I done? Then a prayer to the Only One who can help now.)*

"O, help him, you sweet heavens!"

. . . . . .

"O heavenly powers, restore him!"

. . . . . .

*(But heaven and earth are silent. The only thunder is the voice of one whom she trusted and loved. The words behind that voice are like stinging scorpions. Not a sign of understanding in them, not a sign of tenderness—not a tone of mercy. Hate, accusation, denouncement. The end of the world. Because the world for all of us is the one whom we love. When he is gone the world is gone. When the world is gone we are gone. And therefore we can be calm and empty and oblivious to everything and everyone who a minute ago was so important and powerful. The Creature is alone in her whole being. I can see it in her contracted body and wide open eyes. If there were an army of fathers behind her now, she would be alone. And only to herself would she say those heartbreaking words, the last words of a sound mind, that tries desperately to verify all that happened a second ago. It is unbelievably painful. It is like the soul parting from the body. The separated words crowd each other, hurry one over the other in a fast-growing rhythm.*

*The voice is hollow. The tears behind it are inade-
quate to accompany that last farewell; the speech is
like a stone falling down, down, into a bottomless
abyss.)*

"O, what a noble mind is here o'erthrown!
  The courtier's, soldier's, scholar's eye, tongue, sword:
  The expectancy and rose of the fair state,
  The glass of fashion and the mould of form,
  The observ'd of all observers,—quite, quite down!
  And I, of ladies most deject and wretched,
  That suck'd the honey of his music vows,
  Now see that noble and most sovereign reason,
  Like sweet bells jangled, out of tune and harsh;
  That unmatch'd form and feature of blown youth
  Blasted with ecstasy: O, woe is me,
  To have seen what I have seen, see what I see!"

*(She sinks down on her knees, exhausted, staring
into the blackness of the empty house right at me,
without seeing, without registering anything. Madness
next would be the inevitable and logical madness of
the mind which has lost its world.)*

\* \* \* \*

*(She snaps out of it all, jumps up from the ground,
rubs her head and shakes out her golden hair with her
hands, swerves around and says in her youthful voice)*

THE CREATURE: Well, that's my best, and as Gordon Craig says 'It's just too bad that someone's best
is so bad.'

*(She giggles. Another sign of a trained actor. It doesn't matter how deep emotion is in acting, with the return to life it snaps off and is laid aside with no perturbance.)*

I: Come down here.

*(She vaults over the footlights, runs to the chair next to mine and sits down, tucking her legs under her.)*

I: What do they say to you?

THE CREATURE: . . . . That it is overdone. That I 'tear a passion to tatters'. That nobody would believe me. That it is pathological hypnotism, not acting, and that I will ruin myself and my health. That with this kind of acting nothing is left for the audience's imagination, that for the audience such complete sincerity is embarrassing. As if somebody suddenly appeared naked in the midst of a dressed-up crowd. Is that enough, or is it?

I: Not only enough, but true, my dear.

THE CREATURE: *Et tu, Brute?* You are impossible. I have done everything as you taught me. . . .

I: And done it well, I must say.

THE CREATURE: Then I don't understand; you contradict—

I: Not at all. You have done faithfully everything that I taught you. So far I'm proud of you. So far. Now you must take the next step. It's not an exaggeration when they tell you that you resemble a naked person in a dressed-up crowd. You do. I don't mind it,

73

because I know what it is all about—but the audience will. They are entitled to a finished product.

THE CREATURE: Does that mean more schooling and more exercises?

I: It does.

THE CREATURE: I give up. But go ahead.

I: You don't give up. If I did not tell you right now what I'm going to tell you, you would work until you found it out for yourself. It might take you a few years, maybe more. But you would work until you had mastered the next step. And even then you would not stop. A new difficulty would arise, and you would go after that.

THE CREATURE: Endlessly?

I: Endlessly and persistently. That is the only difference between an artist and a shoemaker. When the shoemaker has done his pair of boots, it is over, he forgets about them. When an artist finishes a piece of work, it is not done. It is just another step. All the steps dovetail one into the other.

THE CREATURE: If you were not so exasperatingly logical; just like an old mathematician, one, two, three, four. Disgusting. No art, just a handicraft. An old cabinet maker, that's what you are.

I: You mean emotion maker? Thank you for the compliment. Would you like me now to turn into a dressmaker and dress your emotions? Because, as we both agree, myself and your superiors, your emotions are quite naked, my child. Quite distressingly so.

74

THE CREATURE: *(Laughs heartily and provocatively.)* I don't mind.

I: But I do. I don't want anybody to say that my pseudo-moralities are immoral. Amoral, maybe, but not immoral.

THE CREATURE: *(Still laughing)* I wouldn't think of such a thing. Please dress me. I'm naked—ears, nose, eyes, emotions and all.

I: I'll take care only of the emotions, if you please. And I'll start by covering them with praise. I noted carefully everything you did in building your part—your physical control, your concentration, your choice and clear outline of emotions, your power of projecting those emotions. All that was splendid. I'm proud of you. But it lacked one thing.

THE CREATURE: What?

I: Characterization.

THE CREATURE: Oh, that's simple. When I put my costume on, and my make-up.

I: Nothing will happen, my dear.

THE CREATURE: You can't say that. When I am all made up and dressed, I feel like the person I am supposed to represent. I'm not myself then. I never worry about characterization, it comes by itself.

*(I must use a strong medium to bring her down from her high horse and heresy. I reach into my pocket for a small ancient book, and open to the first page.)*

I: Read it.

THE CREATURE: One of your tricks?

I: *(Striking a light)* Read it.

THE CREATURE: *(Reads)* *"The Actor: A Treatise on the Art of Playing.* London. Printed for R. Griffiths, at the Dunciad in St. Paul's Church-yard MDCCL."

I: *(I turn a few pages.)* Remember that MDCCL. Almost 200 years, that ought to impress you. Now read here.

THE CREATURE: *(Reads with difficulty the ancient letters and spelling.)* "The actor who is to express to us a peculiar passion and its effects, if he wou'd play his character with *truth,* is not only to assume the emotions which that passion wou'd produce in the generality of mankind; but he is to give it that peculiar form——"

I: *(Interrupting)* Now read louder and remember—

THE CREATURE: *(Does so)* "under which it wou'd appear, when exerting itself in the breast of such a person as he is giving us the portrait of."

*(A pause. The dear Creature slowly raises her beautiful eyes, takes out a cigarette, lights it from my lighter and blows it out furiously. I know that she will listen now.)*

THE CREATURE: Well, what does he mean, that 200-year old anonym?

I: *(Not without a slight triumph)* That before you

76

put on your dress and your make-up you must master your characterization.

THE CREATURE: *(Puts her arm under mine, and says tenderly)* Tell me, how? *(One cannot be angry with her.)* And if you want a cigarette, I'll give you one.

I: *(As if telling a long forgotten fairy tale)* It is like this, my child. The actor creates the whole length of a human soul's life on the stage every time he creates a part. This human soul must be visible in all its aspects, physical, mental and emotional. Besides, it must be unique. It must be *the soul*. The same soul the author thought of, the one the director explained to you, the one you brought to the surface from the depths of your being. No other but that one.

And the character who owns this created soul on the stage is unique and different from all the rest. It is Hamlet and nobody else. It is Ophelia and nobody else. They are human, that is true, but here the similarity ends. We are all human, we have the same number of arms and legs and our noses are placed respectively in the same positions. Yet, as there are no two oak leaves alike, there are no two human beings alike. And when an actor creates a human soul in the form of a character, he must follow the same wise rule of Nature and make that soul unique and individual.

THE CREATURE: *(In self-defence)* Haven't I done that?

I: You have done it in a general way. From your own body, mind and emotions, you created an image which could have been any young girl's image. Sincere, convincing, powerful, but abstract. It could have been Lisa, Mary, Ann. But it was not Ophelia. The body was that of a young girl, but not Ophelia's. The mind was that of a young girl, but not Ophelia's. It was . . .

THE CREATURE: All wrong. What shall I do now?

I: Don't despair. You have conquered more difficult things, this is comparatively easy.

THE CREATURE: *(Satisfied)* All right. What kind of a body had Ophelia?

I: How do I know? You tell me. Who was she?

THE CREATURE: The daughter of a courtier.

I: Which means?

THE CREATURE: Well bred, well controlled, well . . . fed?

I: You don't have to worry about the last, but don't forget the historical elements. A body with the bearing of a chosen creature, with the power and dignity of one born to represent the best of her kind. Analyze now in detail the posture of your head, go to the galleries or look into books. Look at Van Dyck, look at Reynolds. Your arms and hands were natural and sincere, but I could have told you right away that those hands play tennis, drive a car, and, when necessary, can broil a marvelous steak. Study the hands of

Botticelli, of Leonardo, of Raphael. Then your walk
—almost masculine.

THE CREATURE: Well, pictures don't walk.

I: Go and see the procession of nuns in the chapel
on Easter night. If you must see everything.

THE CREATURE: I know. But how do I perceive all
that and incorporate it into the part?

I: Very simply. By studying and making it your
own. By entering into its spirit. Study the different
hands. Understand their weakness, their flower-like
tenderness, their narrowness, their flexibility. You can
control your muscles. Just curl your palm longwise.
Do you see how much narrower it is? Two days
practice and you won't even think about it, but
whenever you want it, it will stay like that as long
as you wish. And when, with that kind of hand, you
grasp your heart, it will be a different gesture than
the one you made. It will be Ophelia's hand clutching
Ophelia's heart, not Miss So-and-So's hand grasping
Miss So-and-So's heart.

THE CREATURE: Can I study and interpret just
one picture or can I use different ones?

I: Not only different ones, but living, contemporary
personalities as well, in the whole or in part. You can
borrow a head from Botticelli, a posture from Van
Dyck, use the arms of your sister and the wrists of
Angna Enters (the last not as a dancer but as a person). The clouds driven by the wind can inspire your

79

walk. And all of this will make a composite creature, just as a tabloid makes a composite photograph of a person or event from a dozen different photographs.

THE CREATURE: When is one supposed to do this?

I: As a rule, the last two or three days of rehearsal, right at the stage where you are now. Not before you are well settled in the part, and know its structure well. But there are exceptions. Some actors prefer to start with characterization. It is more difficult, that is all. And the result is not so subtle, the choice of elements not so wise as it might be if you followed the inward thread of the part first. It is like buying a dress without being measured.

THE CREATURE: How do you make those things acceptable to your own nature? How do you blend them all together? What do you do to make them represent one real, believable person?

I: Let me answer you with questions. How did you acquire your good manners? How did you learn to eat with a knife and fork, to sit straight, to keep your hands quiet? How did you adjust yourself last winter to short skirts and this winter to long ones? How do you know how to walk on the golf course in one way and on the ballroom floor in another? How do you learn to use your voice in your own room in one way and in a taxicab in another? All those and hundreds of small changes make you what you are, so far as your physical personality is concerned. And for all those things you drew living examples from the life which surrounds you. What I propose is the same thing, done professionally. That means organized study and the appropriation, through intensive practice, of all the elements which will make you, in your part, a distinct and unique physical personality.

THE CREATURE: That is why you told me at the very beginning of our talks that I must have absolute control of every muscle in my body so that I would be able to learn quickly and remember all those things?

I: Exactly! 'Learn quickly and remember,' because to acquire good manners you have a lifetime; to create your part physically but a few days.

THE CREATURE: How about mind?

I: Characterization of the mind in the part on the stage is largely a question of the rhythm. The rhythm of thought, I should say. It does not so much concern your character as it concerns the author of that character, the author of the play.

THE CREATURE: Do you mean to say that Ophelia should not think?

I: I wouldn't be so rude as that, but I would say that Shakespeare did all the thinking for her. It is his mind at work which you should characterize while acting Ophelia, or for that matter, any Shakespearean character. The same goes for any author who has a mind of his own.

THE CREATURE: I never thought of that. I always tried to think the way I imagined the character would think.

I: That is a mistake which almost every actor commits. Except geniuses—who know better. The most powerful weapon of an author is his mind. The quality of it, the speed, alertness, depth, brilliancy. All of that counts, without regard to whether he is writing words of Caliban or those of Jeanne d'Arc, or those of Osvald. A good writer's fool is no more foolish than his creator's mind, and a prophet no more wise than the man who conceived him. Do you remember *Romeo and Juliet?* Lady Capulet says about Juliet 'She's not fourteen'. And then a few pages later Juliet speaks.

> "My bounty is as boundless as the sea,
>   My love as deep; the more I give to thee,
>   The more I have, for both are infinite."

Confucius could have said that, or Buddha, or St. Francis. If you will try acting Juliet's part in a way which characterizes her mind as a fourteen-year-old mind, you'll be lost. If you try to make her older you'll ruin Shakespeare's theatrical conception which is that of a genius. If you try to explain it by the early maturity of Italian women, by the wisdom of the Italian Renaissance, and so forth, you will be all tangled up in archaeology and history, and your inspiration will be gone. All you have to do is to grasp the characterization of Shakespeare's mind and follow it.

THE CREATURE: How would you describe the quality of it?

I: A mind of lightning-like speed. Highly concentrated, authoritative, even in moments of doubt. Spontaneous, the first thought is always the last one. Direct and outspoken. Don't misunderstand me, I'm not trying to describe or explain Shakespeare's mind. No words can describe it. All I am trying to do is to tell you that whatever character of Shakespeare you perform, its mind (not yours but the character's) must have those qualities in its manifestation. You don't have to think like Shakespeare, but the outward quality of thinking must be his. It is like portraying an acrobat. You don't have to know how to stand on your head, but all the movements of your body must convey the idea that you are able to turn somersaults whenever you wish to do it.

THE CREATURE: Would you say the same if I had to act in a Bernard Shaw play?

I: Precisely. More so in Shaw's case. His peasants, clerks and girls think like scholars, his saints and kings and bishops like lunatics and monsters. Your portrayal of Shavian character would be incomplete unless the mind of that character, embodied in its ways, continued attack and defence, continued provocation for argument, right or wrong.

THE CREATURE: Sort of an Irish mind.

83

I: There you are. You have explained it much better than I.

THE CREATURE: How do you apply that practically to a part?

I: As I have told you before, it is mostly the rhythm or organized energy of your delivery of the author's words. After studying him and rehearsing him for a length of time, you ought to know the movement of the author's thoughts. They must affect you. You must like them. Their rhythm must infect yours. Try to understand the author. Your training and nature will take care of the rest.

THE CREATURE: Can you apply the same rule of characterization to the emotions of a character?

I: Oh, no. The emotion of a character is the only sphere where the author should pay attention to the actor's demands and adjust his writings to the actor's interpretation. Or, an actor is justified in adjusting the author's writing to achieve the best results for his own emotional outline of the part.

THE CREATURE: Don't say that aloud. All the authors will murder you.

I: The wise ones won't. Emotion is God's breath in a part. Through emotion, the author's characters stand alive and vital. The wise author does everything to make this part of creation in the theatre as harmonious as possible, without ruining the idea and purpose of the play. Gilbert Emery told me that he threw out two and a half pages from his play *Tarnish,* in a big scene between Ann Harding and Tom Powers. He did it because Ann Harding could bring herself and the audience to tears much better by simply listening silently, than by answering every speech of Powers with another speech of the same importance. Gilbert Emery chose wisely between the emotion of an actress and his writing. Clemence Dane gave me permission to cut out every superfluous word in *Granite* for stage presentation. No, the authors won't murder me. They know that you, and I, and all like us work for them in the theatre.

THE CREATURE: But emotions must be characterized just as clearly as body and mind. What is the proper way to do that?

I: When you have mastered the general human emotions in the part, as you have in your Ophelia, when you know when and why anger comes, or pleading, sorrow, joy or despair, whatever the case demands, when it is all clear to you, start to look for one fundamental quality: freedom in expressing your emotions. Absolute, unlimited freedom and ease. That freedom will be your characterization of the emotions at hand. When the inward structure of your part is well prepared and built, when you have mastered its outward appearance, when the manifestation of the thoughts of your character is in perfect accord with the author's way of thinking, watch during rehearsals to see when and where your emotions rise and flame with difficulty. Look for reasons. There may be many. Your fundamentals may not be strong, you may not understand the action. You may be physically uncomfortable, the words may disturb you—their quality or quantity—the movement may distract you, you may be lacking in the means of expression. Find the reason for yourself and eliminate it. Let me give you an example. What scene in Ophelia do you feel least comfortable in?

THE CREATURE: The third act, the performance scene.

I: All right. What is the action?

THE CREATURE: To be insulted.

I: Wrong. To preserve your dignity. Ophelia is a courtier's daughter. The Prince of the reigning house is making unsuitable remarks to her publicly. He is master of her life, the more because she loves him. He can do whatever he pleases. But even if it pleases him to kill her, she will die with the dignity appropriate to her state. Your main action is not to break down, not to show weakness, or to *display publicly your intimate emotion*. Don't forget, the whole court watches Ophelia. Take all that now as your action. Can you find it in yourself easily?

THE CREATURE: Yes.

I: Is the rest all right? Are you comfortable in your seat? Do words come easily into your mind? Are

you vital enough to think with Shakespearean bold-
ness?

THE CREATURE: Yes, yes. I have it. Let me do it
for you.

*(Suddenly behind our backs a voice arises. An old,
shaky, but trained and rich voice, trembling with the
expectation of something big, decisive, half absent
from its own sound.)*

"Lady, shall I lie in your lap" . . .

*(I turn around. The old doorman is standing behind
us.)*

THE CREATURE: *(Like a frozen sea. Calm and terrific in its rigidity.)* "No, my lord."

THE DOORMAN: *(Still tense with expectation, but
I can sense a trace of sorrow and pity toward the beloved one.)* "I mean, my head upon your lap."

THE CREATURE: *(You are my master. You are
within your rights.)* "Aye, my lord."

THE DOORMAN: *(The pain is behind that voice
now. He must go on with assumed madness. He must
hurt one he doesn't want to hurt, to convince the
others.)* "Do you think I meant country matters?"

THE CREATURE: *(The apotheosis of dignity. If I
have to die, I will think nothing, my lord.)* "I think
nothing, my lord."

*(A few speeches more, and the scene is finished.
Fast, terrific, tense. Just right. The Creature jumps
from the seat and whirls along the aisle.)*

THE CREATURE: I have it, I have it now! It's so simple. I felt easier than ever before. It's just nothing.

THE DOORMAN: *(His sad old eyes blinking at her)* It's nothing, Miss—when you know it.

THE CREATURE: Oh, Pa, you were very good. How do you happen to know all the cues?

THE DOORMAN: I have played with all the big players for the last forty years. I have played almost every part in all the big plays. I studied them all, I worked hard. But I did not have time to perfect myself or to think about all the things this gentleman has told you. Now, when I have time to think, and I plunge back into years gone by, I know all my mistakes, and the reasons, and the ways of doing. But there is nothing to apply them to; I try to keep my door shut the best I can. And when I see and hear the young actors struggling, I think always . . . Oh, if youth knew, and if age could do, what a wonderful world it would be. I have enjoyed your talk, sir. Everything was true, very true.

I: I am honored, sir.

THE DOORMAN: Now begging your pardon, would you please take your leave, sir. It's time for rehearsal. *(He finishes with a sly, dreamy smile which covers his old face with wrinkles.)*

>"The actors are come hither, my lord—
>The best actors in the world . . ."

# THE FIFTH LESSON

## *Observation*

We are having tea, the Creature's Aunt, "who knew Mr. Belasco personally", and myself. We are expecting the Creature at any moment. The tea is excellent.

THE AUNT: I think it charming of you to take such an interest in my niece. The child is so absorbed in the theatre. Especially now that she is successful. Can you imagine, she is getting a regular salary. I never thought it possible in the theatre.

I: Just the law of supply and demand.

THE AUNT: I must confess, I don't understand what she wants from you now. She is a "professional".

She has received good notices. She has a good part. What else can she ask? Not that I don't enjoy the pleasure of your company, now and then. And I'm sure my niece does. We both adore the theatre and its people. The late Mr. Belasco—what a charming man he was—said to me once when I considered taking a part in one of his productions "Madame, you belong to opening nights. Your presence in an orchestra seat is just as vital to the play's success as the best performance of all my actors." It was so cute of him. The man was a genius. Would you believe that I never miss an opening night of a successful play?

I: It's very kind of you, Madame.

THE AUNT: Not at all. I'm doing everything to promote—*(she almost sings it. . . . The tea is unbearably hot.)* a b-e-a-u-t-i-f-u-l art of the theatre. Shakespeare. . . . Noel Coward. . . . And what an actor Alexander Woollcott has turned out to be.

I: He has studied hard, Madame.

THE AUNT: Unquestionably. And in the right way. He watched actors for years. He remembered their tricks. Then he took a part and started to act it. Now, if he would just act and act every day as much as he could, he would be remarkable.

*(I gulp the tea which, for some reason, gets hotter and hotter. I am preparing to ask for another cup when the Creature enters. She stops in the middle of*

90

*the room to look us over. There is doubt in her expression.)*

THE CREATURE: And may I ask what you two were talking about?

THE AUNT: About the theatre, my dear, about *(she sings again, and rolls her eyes)* a b-e-a-u-t-i-f-u-l theatre.

THE CREATURE: *(With a slightly grim humor)* Then I hope you agreed.

I: We were getting ready to disagree when you entered. Your Aunt, my dear, just made the statement that all that is necessary to become an actor is to act, act, and act. Am I correct?

THE AUNT: I know that I am right. I don't believe in all the theories and lectures, psychological analyses, and brain-befuddling exercises my niece has told me about. You'll have to forgive me; I'm a straightforward person. And I adore the theatre. But my theory is: To be an actor one must act. So act all you can,—as long as it pays. When it doesn't pay,—stop acting. And that's that. If one has talent, like this child here, . . .

THE CREATURE: Auntie. . . .

THE AUNT: That's all right, my dear. Talent needs advertising like everything else. If one has talent the pay will last for a long time.

I: I'm glad, Madame, you give talent such a boost. But, if I may ask, don't you consider that talent needs cultivation, that only through cultivation can one discover the presence of talent?

THE CREATURE: *(Picking up my thought heartily)* Auntie, dear, it's just like a wild apple and a cultivated apple. They are both apples, but one is green, hard and sour, and the other red, soft, sweet and fragrant.

THE AUNT: To argue with poetical comparisons is unfair, my dear. An apple is one thing. . . .

I: *(Continuing quickly)* And talent another. You are quite right. Let's not compare. Let's have a pleasant teatime. May I ask for another cup? Thank you. *(I receive a full cup of delightful tea, with cream and sugar, then I continue.)* May I ask you, Madame, if you ever heard of a new delightful game which is played much in German Kindergartens, called *Achtungspiele?*

THE AUNT: No, what is it?

I: A very simple game. The teacher makes the children repeat snatches of their activities, things they have done today, yesterday, a few days ago. It serves the purpose of developing the pupil's memory, analyzing his actions, and sharpening his sense of observation. Sometimes the child is allowed to make its own choice, and then the teacher makes her conclusion as to what direction the child's interest takes, and either develops it or warns the parents and other teachers about it. For instance, the child who chooses to remember how it destroyed a bird's nest is not punished, but an effort is made to shift its interest into a different sphere.

THE AUNT: *(Like a glacier)* Very interesting.

I: Oh, not half as interesting as when you try it on the grown-ups. Interesting because it shows how little we grown-ups use a wonderful natural gift, the ability for observation. Would you believe that very few persons can remember how they have acted for the last twenty-four hours?

THE AUNT: Incredible. I can tell you exactly what I have done for the last twenty-four years.

I: Oh, yes, you could *tell* me, I'm sure. But the game is not to tell but silently to perform, to re-enact. Silence helps concentration and brings out hidden emotions.

THE AUNT: I could do it silently if I wanted to. Though I'm not so sure that I would want to. I'm a straightforward, outspoken person.

I: Why not try? It's just a childish game. Would you be willing?

THE AUNT: Oh, I'll try anything.

I: Splendid. We all will try. Let us start on something easy. For instance, . . . for instance, may I ask you to re-enact the process of serving me with that delightful cup of tea which I received from your hands a minute ago,—

THE AUNT: How ridiculous. *(She laughs heartily.)*

A very cute idea. You want me really to go back to Kindergarten.

I: Not at all, Madame. It's just a game. The next test will be mine or your talented niece's.

THE CREATURE: Oh, please, Auntie, I'm curious.

THE AUNT: All right. It's a gloomy afternoon anyhow. Now observe me. *(She begins like a high priestess or Macbeth's witch, almost rolling back her sleeves.)* Here is the cup . . . *(I interrupt.)*

I: Silently, please. No words, just actions.

THE AUNT: Oh, yes, I forgot. The mystery of silence. *(She is a sarcastic old lady. But she has made up her mind, and she is going to show us up—she begins. Her forehead is wrinkled. The thoughts are working. She takes a cup in her right hand, reaches for a teapot with her left. Realizes her blunder, exclaims candidly "Oh, my God", puts the cup back, takes the teapot in her right hand, holds it in the air. I whisper between two sips of tea—)*

I: Don't touch anything, please. Just go through the actions. . .

THE AUNT: I'm doing that exactly.

I: Then kindly put down the teapot.

THE AUNT: Oh, yes. *(She puts it down and lays both hands on the table. Jerks them off immediately, and with maddening speed indicates the motions of taking the cup and pouring a drop of tea into it. Then without placing the pot on the table adds imaginary cream and lemon from respective containers, and*

*hands me the cup by its handle, obviously having for-*
*gotten the saucer and the sugar. The Creature shrieks*
*in unrestrained laughter, and throwing her arms*
*around her Aunt's neck, kisses her many times. I finish*
*my cup of tea.)*

THE AUNT: It's just silly, that's all.

I: No, Madame. It's just an uncultivated gift of observation. Will you allow your niece to re-enact *your* actions of the same event? And as you know, she couldn't foresee that I would choose this particular one. So she will have to do her best unprepared, please.

THE CREATURE: Can I tell it? I'm so excited,—at you and Auntie getting along so nicely, that I couldn't possibly keep silent.

I: Yes, you can tell it, because it's somebody else's action. If it were your own I would insist on your re-enacting it in silence. The gift of observation must be cultivated in every part of your body, not only in your sight, and memory.

THE CREATURE: Auntie, when B. asked you for a cup of tea, you smiled at him. Then you looked at the teapot as if trying to make sure that there was any more tea, then you looked at me and smiled again as if saying "Isn't he cute?"

THE AUNT: *(Booms loudly)* I did not.

I: You did, Madame. I remember it well. It was my only encouragement from you.

THE CREATURE: Then you looked again at B. as if

95

waiting for him to hand you his cup. But he did not.

I: I'm sorry.

THE CREATURE: Then you held your wide right sleeve with your left hand and reached over to the tray for a fresh cup. Took it, holding it on the saucer, and placed it in front of you. Then, still holding your sleeve, you took the teapot. It was quite heavy, so you put it down and got a better grip on the handle. Brought it over the cup, let your sleeve go, took the strainer,—placing it over the cup. Then, holding the cover of the teapot with the fingers of your left hand, you started to pour the tea. The cover was hot and you changed your fingers one after another. When the teacup was three-quarters full, you placed the teapot nearer to you and smiled again, this time at nobody in particular. Then you poured cream with your right hand and dropped in two lumps of sugar, holding the tongs in your left. You handed the cup to B. and placed the tongs on a dish with lemon, right where you can see them now.

THE AUNT: *(Seriously offended)* One would think you were in the theatre, you must have studied me.

I: No. Please don't be cross. I assure you there was no premeditation. *(I turn to the Creature.)* You forgot to mention that your Aunt could not find the cream right away, and for a fraction of a second looked all over the table for it.

THE CREATURE: Yes, and you were playing with your napkin all the time.

THE AUNT: *(Laughs heartily. She is a good sport, after all.)* Aha! So you didn't escape scrutiny either.

I: I didn't try to, Madame. I was intently watching your niece exercising her gift of observation.

THE AUNT: And you taught her that childish game just to watch her pranks.

I: Madame, I did not teach her anything. We both work in the theatre. And the theatre is one place where teaching and preaching are absolutely excluded. Practice is what counts, and only practice.

THE AUNT: Just what I say. Act! act! and you'll be an actor.

I: No. To act is the final result of a long procedure, Madame. Practice everything which precedes and leads toward this result. When you act, it is too late.

THE AUNT: *(Caustically)* And what, if I may ask, has that gift of observation to do with acting, if you please?

I: A great deal. It helps a student of the theatre to notice everything unusual and out of the ordinary in every-day life. It builds his memory, his storage memory, with all visible manifestations of the human spirit. It makes him sensitive to sincerity and to make-believe. It develops his sensory and muscular memory, and facilitates his adjustment to any business he may be required to do in a part. It opens his eyes to the full extent in appreciation of different personalities and values in people and works of art. And lastly, Madame, it enriches his inner life by full and extensive consumption of everything in outward life.

It has the same effect that one banana and a handful of rice, as a day's food, have on a Hindu follower of Yoga. Consumed rightly, getting the maximum energy out of that miserable amount of vitamins, that food gives to a Hindu immeasurable energy, spiritual power, and vitality. We consume a steak at lunch, and imagine at dinnertime that we are hungry. We go through life in the same manner. We think that we see everything, and we don't assimilate anything. But in the theatre, where we have to re-create life, we can't afford that. We are obliged to notice the material with which we work.

THE AUNT: So you tell my niece to notice how her Aunt pours a cup of tea, and then you both make fun of her. *(I see a twinkle in her eye; she is a good sport.)*

THE CREATURE: Oh, Auntie, dear, not at all. He was just joking.

THE AUNT: I know a joke when I see it. He is darn serious, and so am I.

I: No, you are not. Otherwise I wouldn't read in your eyes the invitation to continue. You are amused. I appreciate that. I cannot teach, but I will endeavor to amuse you. Your gift of observation will do the rest.

## OBSERVATION

THE AUNT: *(Graciously)* If you want another cup of tea, pour it yourself.

I: Thank you. *(I do it, and Auntie watches me like a hawk. After I am through—)* Madame, I realize that for the first time you have given me your full attention. I'll make use of it. You adore the theatre. We, your niece and I, work for the theatre and in the theatre. When you go to an opening night, you go out shopping and choose the most suitable dress. We shop in life every day and choose the most suitable things for every night that we spend in the theatre. To us, they are all opening nights. They all command us to be at our best. The actor who has his gift of observation dulled and inactive will appear in worn-out dress on a gala occasion. As a rule, I believe that inspiration is the result of hard work, but the only thing which can stimulate inspiration in an actor is constant and keen observation every day of his life.

THE AUNT: Do you mean to say that great actors walk through life spying on all their acquaintances, relatives and passers-by?

I: I'm afraid they do, Madame. Besides, they spy on themselves, too.

THE CREATURE: How otherwise could we know what we can do and what we can't?

THE AUNT: We are speaking about *great* actors, my child.

THE CREATURE: Oh, poor me, poor me. What a

blow. *(She pouts humorously.)* Auntie, are you through with advertising me?

THE AUNT: You are a spoiled creature.

I: She is a marvelous creature. Allow me to advertise her a little. I won't overdo it. I'll tell you only how we both developed, and made important observations in our craft. Your niece had the part of the blind girl in *The Cricket on the Hearth*. She rehearsed it well, but nobody ever believed that she was blind! She came to me and we went out to find a blind man. We found one on the Bowery. He sat at the corner. He did not move for four hours. We waited for him to go because we wanted to see him walking,— finding his way. To ask him to move wouldn't be good. He would be self-conscious. For the sake of art we risked hunger, pneumonia (it was chilly), loss of time.

Finally the beggar got up and went home. We followed him there, it took another hour, gave him a dollar for his involuntary service to us, and left highly enriched in experience. But the price of it, not counting even the dollar, was too big. In the theatre, one cannot spend four hours waiting for beggars. One must pick up and store experiences for all emergencies at all times. One must start from the beginning so. . . .

THE CREATURE: I decided, Auntie, on a plan, and B. approved of it.

I: Exactly. Go ahead and tell it, it's your contribution.

THE CREATURE: I decided that for three months, from twelve to one every day, wherever I happened to be and whatever I might be doing, I would observe everything and everybody around me. And from one to two, during my lunch time, I would recall the observations of the previous day. If I happened to be alone I would re-enact, like the German children, my own past actions.

I do not do it any more except occasionally, but in three months' time I became as rich in experiences as Croesus in gold. At first I tried to jot them down, now I don't even need to do that. Everything registers automatically somewhere in my brain, and through the practice of recalling and re-enacting I'm ten times as alert as I was. And life is so much more wonderful. You don't know how rich and wonderful it is.

THE AUNT: You ought to change your career, my child. You ought to become a detective.

I: Madame, isn't every produced play and every acted part a discovery of hidden values and treasures? The unveiling of virtues and vices, the control of passions? A fourth wall removed from a room? A battlefield exposed? The grave of "Poor Yorick" dug out?

THE AUNT: Well, well, well. *(Not entirely convinced)* Still, somehow, it doesn't sound real to me.

Very theoretical. Bookish. In my estimation the ways of the theatre, and all other arts for that matter, ought to be natural. We don't do those things in life.

I: Forgive me, let's drop the subject. Your niece tells me your sister has just come back from abroad. Did you find her rested, looking well, when you met her at the pier?

THE AUNT: Oh, yes, thank you. She was rested all right, but as for looks!—That woman will be the death of me! She is the champion worst dresser in New York. Can you imagine; she had on a beige Eugenie hat with a dull mauve plume. And a narrow purple satin ribbon flecked with silver. Even tiny silver marcasite clasps on the side. She wore a travelling outfit of checked velveteen—small checks, first a brown line, then a grey, then a purple, on a background of a dull mocha color. . . .

I: *(Interrupting rudely)* Madame, what you have said just now shows a gift of observation, cultivated and used quite naturally in real life. In the theatre we do the same thing, making our circle of observation as wide as possible. We use everything, and everybody, as an object, the only difference being that we never talk about it, we act it.

THE AUNT *(Sighs softly, and changes the subject of the conversation to the Horse Show at Madison Square Garden. We finish tea in peace and mutual agreement. The Creature is silent and thoughtful.)*

# THE SIXTH LESSON

## *Rhythm*

*The Creature put it to me bluntly.*

THE CREATURE: If you have any longing for beauty you'll go with me and see it.

I: The only time I indulge in a longing for beauty is between seven and eight in the morning. . . .

THE CREATURE: *(Even more bluntly)* I'll be at your door tomorrow morning at seven-fifteen.

\*     \*     \*     \*

*At twenty minutes to eight today the Creature and I find ourselves standing at the top of the Empire State Building. Far below, innumerable arms of stone are desperately reaching for the sky. In the distance, the same sky is gently descending towards green fields and a pearly sea but they seem to make no effort to reach it. The Creature and I are most entertainingly silent. After a while we sit down.*

I: I'm certainly grateful to you.

THE CREATURE: I knew you would like it. . . . *(Suddenly, very shrewdly)* . . . And I knew you would explain it to me. You will have to explain it to yourself anyhow; that is, if you register "all this" emotionally the way I do.

I: Suppose I am not able to explain? And suppose I register "all this" emotionally quite differently from you?

THE CREATURE: Exactly what I hope will happen.

I: May I ask why?

THE CREATURE: You may. First, because if you are not able to explain a thing you always lean on me for support, proof or clarification. I am your "Exhibit A." This makes me feel important and wise. A marvelous feeling, almost like receiving a fan letter. I think I'll be able to help you—this time as usual. *(In her gaze I feel a deal of pride and gratitude. Well hidden though, behind a youthful challenge.)* Second, if you feel anything differently we will plunge into an argument—and I rather think you profit by my arguments. As a matter of fact, without my arguments, I cannot imagine what you would do. *(She must be happy. She is positively defiant today.)*

I: Probably I would invent arguments.

THE CREATURE: An extremely difficult and dangerous procedure. You might not be able to invent them and even if you did, they might not be real and convincing. It is only human to be prejudiced toward one's own arguments.

I: It is only human to be prejudiced toward arguments used against us, as well.

THE CREATURE: Yes, but that kind of prejudice is an incentive for one's own strength and convictions. Isn't it?

I: In life, yes. And in the arts, the straightest and most practical answer is also yes—especially in the theatre.

THE CREATURE: Is that because on the stage, resistance and conflict of actions are the essential elements of its life?

I: Precisely. Suppose in the first act of *The Merchant of Venice*, Antonio should pay the money on the dot, change his religion and ask for the hand of Jessica. . . . Don't laugh. I am serious. That is an exaggerated example. Here is a legitimate one:

"How all occasions do inform against me,
And spur my dull revenge!
      . . . Rightly to be great
Is not to stir without great argument,
But greatly to find quarrel in a straw
When honour's at the stake."

Which is *Hamlet*—Act IV, Scene IV. All through Shakespeare you can find those marvelous sign posts for the actor. They are wisely concealed in the text of the plays—not displayed in a multitude of boastful directions. In those two lines—the first which come to mind—you see the straightest advice: No action without conflict!

THE CREATURE: And is that stimulant of action the sole secret of a successful play or acting?

I: Oh, no. This is only a theoretical beginning. An A. B. C. so to speak. In the theatre I call it "Mr. What"—rather a deadly personality without his mate, "How". It is only when "How" appears on the stage that things begin to happen. The conflict of actions may be *presented* on the stage and remain there petrified awaiting an answer to the question: "What is the theme of the play?" In which case it is not theatre. But the same conflict may be *created* with unexpected spontaneity, with uncalculated impulse and it will plunge the audience into a feverish state of partisanship toward one side or another. It will force them to find their own living and excited answer. This will be theatre. And the secret is not in the question: "What is the theme of the play?" but in the statement: "This is how the theme perseveres or does not persevere through all obstacles."

THE CREATURE: You are, of course, speaking about what happens in performance itself when you mention the "unexpected spontaneity and uncalculated impulse". You don't mean during the preparation of the play and the working rehearsals. You have always told me that inspiration and spontaneity are results of calculation and practice.

I: I am still inclined to believe so. I am speaking about the performance itself.

THE CREATURE: All right. Now I want an explanation from you. Why do we stand, for I don't know how long, here on the top of the Empire State Building; silent, awed, bewildered, exhilarated? The view from here is remarkable but not unexpected. I knew it before I actually saw it—from hundreds of photographs and newsreels. I have flown over Manhattan in an airplane; moreover, I live in a twenty-third story penthouse. I have seen it before. Why is the impression so great?

I: Because that remarkable "How" has had a finger in the affair.

THE CREATURE: You seem to be enthusiastic about this "How". I'll be jealous.

I: You may well be. Let me show you "How's" ways and means as opposed to those of "What". "What" would take you from the street level of that boiling, screeching, clanging, arguing city of New York to the window of the first floor of the Empire State Building. He would open the window and say to you, "This, my child, is the first of the hundred and

107

two floors of this building. As you see, the difference between the level commonly known as the street level, and the first floor is slight. Exactly twenty feet. You hear the same noises. You see almost the same view. You do not feel much separation from the squirming mass of humanity below. Let's go to the second floor."

THE CREATURE: *(In horror)* What?

I: "To the second floor, my child," is the answer of "What", and no sooner said than done. You *are* on the second floor. A slight change in the analysis of the height and difference in view follows. Then "What", with appropriate explanations, takes you to the third floor, fourth floor and so on until you reach the hundred and second. . . .

THE CREATURE: Oh, no. I beg your pardon. He does not take me to the fourth floor, and so on.

I: "What" is very persistent, I assure you.

THE CREATURE: That doesn't matter. On the third floor, exactly, I take him gently by the neck and push him over the window-sill toward the level "commonly known as the street level". Curtain.

I: But suppose you did go with him through all the hundred and two floors? Can you imagine your emotions then, in the face of this splendor?

THE CREATURE: I presume there would be none.

I: Why? Where would be the difference? Let us try and find out. You would climb each step logically. You would understand where you were and how high you were. You would realize the gradual change. You would be, as a matter of fact, thoroughly advised on every detail of this remarkable structure. Why do you think there would be no emotion?

THE CREATURE: I really don't know, but I hate the very idea of it.

I: May I ask "How" to bring us here?

THE CREATURE: Please.

I: We are taken along the street. The City rushes to work. No, more than that. It stampedes toward the havens of existence, to the places of its "jobs". "Jobs" which will give to every man in the city— bread, a roof, hope in the daytime, quiet sleep at night. Those things seem as precious to them as black pearls to a diver. Everybody is afraid to miss the time-clock, to lose his work. Terrific tension in steps, gestures, faces and words. There are exactly so many minutes to make so many miles. One cannot stop for a second and compare his own frenzied speed with the serene speed of the sun or wind or sea. To give oneself courage one must shriek and yell and laugh loudly and falsely.

As if not satisfied with that manifestation, all the conceivable means of sound production lash one's eardrums. Rivets, horns, bells, grind of gears and high-pitched groans of brakes, whistles, gongs and sirens—all seem to yell in a steady rhythm, "Go to work—right away. Go to work—right away." It is

like two-fourths time in music repeated endlessly—
with ever increasing volume. We are part of that
rhythm. We walk faster. We breathe faster. Whatever words you say to me, you flash like radio signals.
I answer you with speed. Finally we arrive at the door
of the Empire State Building and we find ourselves
struggling. It is so difficult to tear ourselves away
from the surging currents of arms, legs and faces, and
turn inside. It takes an effort, but we do it.

In a flash we find ourselves in a box of an elevator—
cut off as if with a knife from the world behind. I
could compare that feeling with the *forte fortissimo*
of an orchestra, cut off by the master hand of a con-
ductor, to be resumed by the tender *sostenuto* of vio-
lins. How long it lasts, we do not know. We are alone.
We shoot up through space. We change elevators.
We shoot up again. The upward flash of those hundred and two floors seems like two winks of an eye.
Almost two seconds in silence—in repose. The door
opens. We find ourselves here, suspended from the
sky by man's genius—separated from the earth by the
result of his labor.

Wherever we look, space flows, inviting to the eye
and thought. We are not forced to accept any direction, any command, any limits. We are yanked out
from the measures of Scriabine's *Prelude*, in fifteen-
eighths time, with its torturing temptations, and
thrown suddenly on a broad, streaming magic carpet,

to float in the air to the rhythm of a steady wind which seems to sing out, in measured intervals, one word, "Space". Our spirit is raised in an upward flash from torment to bliss.

THE CREATURE: And "How" is responsible for that upward two-winks-of-an-eye "flash"—which seems to produce such a remarkable result.

I: Aren't you grateful? And don't you realize "How's" importance?

THE CREATURE: Yes. (Slowly thinking) Importance to what?

I: To our profession.

THE CREATURE: Are you serious?

I: As serious as if I were telling you a joke.

THE CREATURE: How do I know—maybe you are. After all, "How"—it's ridiculous.

I: Do you want a learned, much abused, common name for "How"?

THE CREATURE: I'll be delighted.

I: *Rhythm!*

THE CREATURE: *(Her usual, charmingly humorous self)* I've heard the name somewhere—but I've never had the pleasure.

I: Neither had I. Jaques Dalcroze told me a great deal about Rhythm in Music and in Dancing, two arts in which it is the essential and vital element. I found a book on Rhythm in Architecture; it is not translated into English. Those were the only two reliable and practical guides to that great element of every art. Critics occasionally mention rhythm in painting and sculpture, but I have never heard it explained. In the theatre the mechanical word "Tempo" is substituted, but it has nothing to do with Rhythm. If Shakespeare had cast those two, he would have written:

> Rhythm—the Prince of Arts.
> Tempo—his bastard Brother.

THE CREATURE: Splendid. Now I want to know all about both of them.

I: You would never believe the countless hours I spend trying to define Rhythm so that it can be applied to all the arts.

THE CREATURE: Have you succeeded?

I: Not yet. The nearest I have come to it is *the orderly, measurable changes of all the different elements comprised in a work of art—provided that all those changes progressively stimulate the attention of the spectator and lead invariably to the final aim of the artist.*

THE CREATURE: Sounds methodical.

I: Because it is the beginning of a thought. I do not claim that it is a final definition. I beg you to think about it and find a better one. Put it to your friends. I'll be grateful for it. We will all be. Meantime, I would like you to attack mine. It will give me a chance to defend it.

THE CREATURE: All right. You say first: "Orderly and measurable"—but suppose I am creating "Chaos"? How can it be orderly and measurable?

I: You forget the word "changes". Your work of art, "Chaos", if it is such, must consist of a number of conflicting actions. They may be as disorderly as your genius will let them be. But the "changes" from one to another must be orderly. And that is exactly what only a genius can make them. If you remember Michelangelo's frescoes on the ceiling of the Sistine Chapel, you remember that from the floor looking upward they give a perfect impression of "Chaos", prototype of creation. Take a reproduction of those frescoes and spread it before you on the table. One look will be sufficient to convince you that it is "Chaos" composed of the most "orderly and measurable" changes of all the elements involved.

THE CREATURE: I do remember. You are right. But I'll be scrupulous. What do you mean by "changes"? Fluctuations?

I: No, not fluctuations. Precisely changes. Perhaps I can explain myself more clearly by another example. You recall Leonardo's "Last Supper"?

THE CREATURE: I do. Very well, indeed. I studied the movement of all the hands in it. I knew them by heart and could use all of them freely and naturally.

I: Very well then. The element here is *the hand*. It changes its position twenty-six times. Twenty-three visible and three invisible. If you knew all the positions by heart and could freely change from one to another, building up their significance with each change, you would achieve a Rhythm of that particular masterpiece.

THE CREATURE: Isn't that exactly what Isadora Duncan did, and what Angna Enters does now?

I: It is.

THE CREATURE: I see. One more question. On the canvas of the "Last Supper" the hands change, but at the same time they are stationary. How can you apply the word Rhythm to them? Isn't Rhythm applied to movement?

I: There is no limitation. A glacier moves two inches in a century; a swallow flies two miles in a minute—they both have Rhythm. Expand the idea from the glacier to a theoretical standstill and from the swallow to a theoretical light-speed. Rhythm will include and carry them all within its scope. To exist is to have Rhythm.

THE CREATURE: How about its "elements"?

I: That is simple. Tone, movement, form, word, action, color—anything a work of art can be made from.

THE CREATURE: How would you apply "orderly and measurable changes" to colors on canvas?

I: Take Gainsborough's "Blue Boy". The dominating color is blue. It varies an infinite number of times. Each time the change is clean cut and almost imperceptible. It is orderly. Countless copyists have tried to measure the amount of indigo in each change. They generally fail, but that does not mean that it is immeasurable, because it was done once.

THE CREATURE: Continue with the same example. How does the change in blues "stimulate progressively the attention of the spectator"?

I: Simply by arousing his curiosity to look at that which is *not* blue.

THE CREATURE: You mean . . .

I: . . . the pale and refined yellowish-pink face of the "Blue Boy".

THE CREATURE: True. And at the same time it "points to the final aim of the artist", that same boy's face.

I: Must you run ahead of me to the conclusion?

THE CREATURE: I wouldn't be a woman if I didn't love to have the last word.

I: The least I can do is to make you believe you have it.

THE CREATURE: What do you mean by "make me believe"?

I: I have not told you all about Rhythm yet.

THE CREATURE: Oh, that is all right. That only means I'll have many more last words.

I: Let us hope so.

THE CREATURE: I am sure of it. And to prove it to you I will even have a few *first* words. Here is one.

While I was working in the theatre—legitimate theatre, mind you—in stock companies and on Broadway, I found that old reliable "Tempo" very helpful. You abused it a few minutes ago. As a matter of fact, it saved me many times when I did not know what to do. . . .

I: *(Oh, how pleased I am!)* Yes—exactly—when you did not know what to do! You just sped over the embarrassing moments until you knew what to do. Marvelous! I have seen performances when actors apparently never had an idea what to do because all the elements I could discover in three acts were "Tempo" and that other savior of embarrassing moments, "Intonation". *(I pat her on the shoulder humorously.)* My dear friend, stick to last words.

THE CREATURE: You are horrid. In stock, the poor actor often has no time or opportunity to find out what to do.

I: Let him not lie. Let him sketch the situation lightly. Let him glide over it truthfully—then he may, on the spur of the moment, discover what to do. Such things happen in life. You meet somebody you did not know was in town and whom you do not want to meet, and spontaneously you start to act. You get your cue and you answer. After all, that is what the author wants from you. Spontaneous answers to his cues.

THE CREATURE: But where does one get that spontaneity?

# RHYTHM

I: In a developed sense of Rhythm. Not from Tempo, surely, which means slow, medium, fast. That is far too limited. On the other hand, Rhythm has an endless, eternal swing. All created things live by Rhythm, by a transition from one definite thing to another greater one. Take this speech, for instance:

"You lie, in faith; for you are call'd plain Kate,
And bonny Kate, and sometimes Kate the curst;
But, Kate, the prettiest Kate in Christendom,
Kate of Kate-Hall, my super-dainty Kate,
For dainties are all cates; and therefore, Kate,
Take this of me, Kate of my consolation;—
Hearing thy mildness prais'd in every town,
Thy virtues spoke of, and thy beauty sounded,—
Yet not so deeply as to thee belong,—
Myself am mov'd to woo thee for my wife."

And this, as you well know, is *The Taming of the Shrew*—Act II, Scene I. This speech can be the most deadly, monotonous affair, delivered by an actor without a sense of Rhythm. And speed or Tempo won't save him. The faster he goes—the duller he will sound. But I have heard this speech spoken by an actor who knew the value of "changes" from "plain" to "bonny"; from "curst" to "prettiest"; from "Kate-Hall" to "super-dainty"; and so forth. I assure you I never heard a shorter speech in my life. It was an avalanche of changes; a dose of admiration—which is the shortest measurable time in the theatre. The most brilliant test of the difference between "Tempo" and "Rhythm" is the first soliloquy of Claudius in *Hamlet*, which begins:

> "O, my offence is rank, it smells to heaven;
> It hath the primal eldest curse upon't,—
> A brother's murder!—Pray can I not,
> Though inclination be as sharp as will:
> My stronger guilt defeats my strong intent;
> And, like a man to double business bound,
> I stand in pause where I shall first begin,
> And both neglect. . . ."

Study it sometime. Do you see now?

THE CREATURE: I see one thing. More exercises are entering my busy day.

I: Well, the last word is yours—what shall it be?

THE CREATURE: Anything that will enable me to "Stimulate progressively the attention of my spectators".

I: Bravo! You are a willing victim. In that case, the workout will be simple. For an actor, the business of acquiring a sense of Rhythm is a matter of giving himself up freely and entirely to any Rhythm he happens to encounter in life. In other words, not to be immune to the Rhythms which surround him.

THE CREATURE: But to do that, one must know and realize what Rhythm is. Suppose I am Rhythm-deaf or, will you say, unconscious? What should I do?

# RHYTHM

I: "To a nunnery, go; and quickly too. Farewell."

THE CREATURE: Oh, please—I really do think I have no sense of Rhythm.

I: You are mistaken. There is not a stone in the universe without a sense of Rhythm. A few actors, maybe, but very few. Every normal being has it. Sometimes undeveloped, in a dormant state, true. But a little work will bring it forth.

THE CREATURE: Don't torture me now. Tell me how.

I: Do not hurry me. It is one of the hardest subjects to explain because it is so simple and universal. A child is born with the manifestation of Rhythm present. It breathes. A fair start which nature provides for all. After that, development follows. First in walking, second in speech, third in emotions. One step, one word, one emotion changes into another and then another, each with the same allegiance, a final aim in view. This is the first level of Rhythm—consciousness. The second level arrives when outside forces impose their Rhythm on you. When you walk or move or gesture with or for others. When you walk in line; run to meet a friend; shake hands with an enemy. When your words answer other words; sweeping you with them or holding you still. When your emotions are the direct answer and result of somebody else's feelings.

THE CREATURE: What is the third level?

## THE SIXTH LESSON

I: When you command and create your own Rhythm and that of others. It is perfection. It is a result. Do not hurry to achieve it. The student must start with the second level. He must not do much at the start. All that is required of him is to notice these manifestations in real life and store them away in his brain. Special attention should be given to the results of different Rhythms. The best thing to start with is music, where Rhythm is most pronounced. Go to a concert; a street organ, if you prefer, will do just as well. But listen to it with all your being, entirely relaxed and ready to be swept by the definite measures of the music. Give yourself up to the emotions it brings to you. Let them change with the changes in the music. Above all, be attentive and flexible. Follow music with the other arts, these with every-day occurrences.

THE CREATURE: *(In ecstasy, as always when she discovers that two and two are four.)* I know now. That is what has happened to me here, on this height. I gave myself up entirely to the terrific change of Rhythm performed so quickly, so masterfully.

I: So impressively. An elephant would stagger under the effect of that change. No great virtue for you.

THE CREATURE: Very kind of you, dear Sir, but that is not going to be your last word. Suppose after a while I am sensitive to music? Where do I go? To what should I be sensitive next?

# RHYTHM

I: You are already sensitive to a trifling jump of some thousand feet in the air.

THE CREATURE: Please!

I: You are sensitive to the Rhythm of the New York streets. You nearly ran me out of breath.

THE CREATURE: But I won't be sensitive to your humor! It's rather annoying.

I: I am sorry to disappoint you again. *(I suspect that she is serious.)* You *are* sensitive to my humor because you changed the strength of your voice; the speed of your words; the amount of demand in your request. You changed your Rhythm.

THE CREATURE: One day I'll learn to argue with you. Please tell me: what shall I pay attention to after I respond to music freely and easily?

I: *(She pleads so tenderly that I follow my own recipe and change my Rhythm. I take her by the hand and lead her to the balustrade.)* Don't look at me now, my dearest friend, look into space and listen with your inner ear. Music, and the other arts which follow naturally, will be only an open road to the whole of the universe. Don't miss anything in it. Listen to the waves of the sea. Absorb their sweeping change of time, with your body, brain and soul. Talk to them as Demosthenes did, and don't weaken after the first attempt. Let the meaning and Rhythm of your words be a continuation of their eternal sound. Inhale their spirit and feel at one with them, even for an instant. It will make you, in the future, able to portray the eternal parts of universal literature. Go through the same experience with woods, fields, rivers, sky above—then turn to the city and swing your spirit to its sound as you did to its creative rattle. Don't forget the quiet, dreamy, small towns—and above all, don't forget your fellow men. Be sensitive to every change in the manifestation of their existence. Answer that change always with a new and higher level of your own Rhythm. This is the secret of existence, perseverance and activity. This is what the world really is—from the stone up to the human soul. The theatre and the actor enter this picture only as a part. But the actor cannot portray the whole if he does not become a part.

THE CREATURE: *(Very thoughtfully and sadly)* I am mortified.

I: Why?

THE CREATURE: Thinking how busy I shall be for the next few months.

I: Yes. But you will always know "what to do next". Isn't that a consolation?

THE CREATURE: Rather! My regards to "How"! Shall we go?

*(We do. The elevator whisks us down. The street swallows us—and we change our Rhythm.)*